NEW MAN EMERGING

NEW MAN EMERGING

*An Awakening Man's Guide to Living a Life of Purpose,
Passion, Freedom & Fulfillment*

MICHAEL DESANTI

Waterside Press

Printed in the United States of America

First Printing, 2019

ISBN-13: 978-1-943625-13-0 print edition
ISBN-13: 978-1-941768-75-4 ebook edition

Waterside Productions
2055 Oxford Ave
Cardiff, CA 92007
www.waterside.com

TABLE OF CONTENTS

Acknowledgements · vii

Part 1 – Keep Your Death Close · · · · · · · · · · · · · · · · · · · 1

3 Damaging Words · 9

Tapping into the Eternal · 13

The Myth of "One Day" · 17

Question #1 · 21

Our Greatest Poison · 24

Your Comfort Zone is Elastic · 28

Our Current Epidemic · 32

Your Power is Your Presence · 40

Slaying the 3 "D"emons · 44

Organize Your Inner World · 52

Purpose vs. Platform · 75

Part 2 – Chasing Grizzlies · 79

Trust Your Medicine · 83

Channel Your Creativity · 92

What is it All For? · 100

Welcome the War Within · 104

Be Her Hero · 108

Foundations for Fulfillment ·116

Part 3 – The Legacy We Leave · · · · · · · · · · · · · · · · · · · 123

Be the Eagle · 126

The Ultimate Medicine · 131

Find Your Tribe · 136

The Lion and the Fox · 143

Live by Our Promises · 146

Question #2 · 152

Goodbye, for Now · 157

ACKNOWLEDGEMENTS

"If a man can see further it is because he has stood on the shoulders of giants."

- Isaac Newton

The following people are my giants...

First and foremost to my Creator. You who are worshipped in so many ways and in so many names and yet you remain the unnamable One. Thank you for this life, how dare I ask for more.

To my mother, you have been my greatest champion from day one. You were and always are my guiding light of unconditional love. I chose you in this life and will choose you in every other.

To my wife. Whatever good I have done in this life, you are my reward for it. You are my heart, my hero, my home. I am the luckiest man I know.

To my brother Christopher. We were forced to live side-by-side as kids, we chose to live side-by-side now. Thank you for introducing me to a greater world of transformation and for always standing for my greatness. What I have learned from you is beyond measure.

To my brother Donnie. Thank you for introducing me to my medicine. Your impact on me growing up has left an impression on my heart that can never be repaid.

To my sister-in-laws. You are both a gift. Thank you for loving my brothers in a way that no other woman can.

To my trainers and trainer mentors. You have all given me a gift that has forever altered the course of my life. I now live with an un-payable debt that can only be repaid through serving others.

To my coach, Gary Grant of Heroic Life Strategies. The clarities in parts of this book were forged from many of our conversations and the assignments that you invited me to in the exploration of my greater self. Thank you for all the lessons. I am truly grateful for you.

To my friends and my family, old and new. Every single one of you has left an imprint on my heart and my spirit that will echo into eternity. I am who I am because of you all.

Thank you to all of you. You will hear your words and inspirations throughout this text. This book is as much yours as it is mine.

A Gift

This book is dedicated to my soul's equal counterpart, the Divine Feminine. For centuries you have called for peace, screamed from the treetops that a life of beauty is possible and have patiently waited for boys to put down their foolish games that have caused the world heartache and despair. For far too long have you wept at night praying for another way as we men ignored your plea and went on fighting, comparing and competing, only to never be satisfied. In our immaturity we have caused suffering and pain by simply refusing your deeper wisdom and patience and foolishly mistook your vulnerability for weakness. I am as guilty as the rest; and my mistakes and blind spots are far too many to count. I ask for your love and forgiveness as the masculine awakens. This book is dedicated to you. It is my promise, that in our mistakes, there were seeds of wisdom planted that are now emerging. This book is my contract with you that I am putting down my sword and walking off the battlefield completely. I do this not from a defeat of spirit but quite the contrary, but rather, with a clarity of purpose and vision that is fueled by your beauty and love. A commitment to healing the wounds that we have collectively caused by our sleep. This book is a promise. We are awakening. You can rest now. We are coming home to you.

⚜ ⚜ ⚜

PART 1

KEEP YOUR DEATH CLOSE

On April 21, 2015, I held my father's hand as his last breath escaped him. I had lost people close to me before in my life but never in such a dramatic way and never someone that had been so close and influential in molding and shaping me into who I am. He raised me, defined me, challenged me and gave me my name. He instilled in me certain principles and directions that would equate to who I am and how I operate in the world as a man. Parts of me are indisputably his and the space that he filled up in my life was immense.

Although my mood as he passed on wasn't sadness, there was drama, electricity and confusion; all the elements that make up mystery. I remember walking to the window of the ICU and staring out into the wet spring day of New Jersey. The rain from the night before soaked the base of the blossom trees making the bark chocolate dark while the early blossoms were vibrant with young life.

It was a spring day that only the northeast knows. It was the in-between reluctance of nature of whether she should hold on to winter or totally surrender and dive head first into the summer heat. The in-between. Like where I stood at the moment and what I had just witnessed. I noticed as nature didn't even flinch in regard to what just happened. In a breath I just lost my hero, my mentor, one of my best friends, the one and only man that I could call "dad." While I assumed that the world should pause for a moment, Mother Nature disagreed and moved on, she kept to her rhythms and withheld her mysteries of the unseen into which my dad just entered.

For the months that followed I lived with an ache in my heart that is hard to explain and put into words. The gaping hole of my father's presence was truly missed, not in a dramatic way but closer to the mundane every day moment and nuance. My best friend, who had lost his father years before, said to me "now you are part of tribe that must navigate the world without a parent."

In those months and years after, there was a yearning for me to live a life that my father could be proud of. A way to live that life would be to honor him *and his traditions and the love and guidance that he passed down to me. But over time after he passed, there was an insight that haunted me. I share the same fate. One day, not knowing exactly how, my final breath would escape me from the home it made throughout my life; disappearing into the ethers and unknown only to take on a new home for its next magnificent phase. There was a peace that I lived with, one that was fueled by creativity, contribution and urgency. The sadness and mourning of my father's passing began to transform and made room in my heart for ways to honor him by living a life of passion, fulfillment and purpose. If I, we, shared the same fate I became determined that when death came to my door I would be ready. I would have nothing for him to take as his prize. No regrets, no gifts unopened in my heart, no loving words not spoken to the people that deserved them from me, no ideas left unexplored and certainly no love left behind in me for fear of giving it and being misunderstood. In short, I was determined to die on empty. My life, up until this day, has become a purposeful journey of leaving no stone unturned in my spirit that belongs here on earth; leaving me unencumbered to meet my fate one day, ready, hollow, empty and free to fly the day my last breath escapes me.*

There is a New Man Emerging, a committed spirit who dedicates his life to creating the greatest value in his work, relationships and world. He is a man that is dedicated to growth and contribution and to experiencing the greatest version of himself. He is a departure from the old macho, never-show-your-emotions man that is unwilling to explore his inner terrain and unwilling to forgive. The man that is insistent on grudge-holding while the very spirit within him fades and flickers out and is gone long before he dies. The New Man Emerging is also a departure from the spineless man who will pander to every whim of the feminine attraction. The man that is always needing to please the world and his woman; not because it is in the core of his being but rather to make his woman and the world pause, notice him and appreciate him so that he can finally have their approval to move forward and commit to his life's purpose. Meanwhile, decade after decade he continues to wait.

The New Man Emerging is an evolution, a departure from the old. He is a man who is willing, even insistent, on incorporating masculine and feminine principles into his life, marrying his mind and his heart, leading by example and living his life with urgency so that it shakes him to his very core daily. Not only is he unafraid to see and travel the world but he is also committed to exploring the inner universe of his own being. His journey is to discover the uncharted lands of his own heart so as to heal the wounds of a past that keeps him from being fully alive and present.

The purpose of this book is two-fold. First it is to serve as a guide for the evolving man, the man who is committed to awakening so that the world can experience his gifts and his mission in life thereby creating a world that can finally experience peace. It is to unite the tribes of this evolutionary masculine, to create a brotherhood and remind each of you that you are not alone; that there is a tribe waiting for you whose hearts beat to that same drum and whose desire is greater than balancing out the status quo.

And second, this book serves as an invitation, a beckoning call to a new type of warrior, one that is committed to slaying the demons of his own mind while extending seeds of peace to the hearts of his enemies and critics. He is a warrior whose ultimate enemy is his own ego that has him trapped in fear and mediocrity and has him doubting himself, needing others' approval and pretending he is superior by blocking off the very passageways to his emotions. The call is to this warrior whose weapons are his principles, his navigation is his mind and his ultimate goal is to discover the very depths of his heart and inner world, not to conquer it but to share it with those who follow.

This book is the culmination and cultivation of years of coaching thousands of men. Its pages don't contain answers, but rather questions that lead you to your own understanding. This book is not the end point, but the beginning, a doorway in to your own journey of self-discovery. It is an invitation to live from a place of purpose and do the work necessary for the evolution of your own masculine spirit.

The evolving terrain of our culture is changing faster than ever. But the questions facing men remain the same as our oldest ancestors, "Who am I?" and "Why am I here?" From the beginning of time we have asked these two most critical questions. And the few that have had the courage to explore their depths have developed and achieved the freedom and fulfillment of what it means to constantly ask and answer them. They've left us a blueprint of a new possibility for our collective future. As a culture we are breaking free of old paradigms of how we once related to women, politics and economics, globalism and different cultures. Growth and breaking free is not without its discomforts. But now more than ever it is time for the clear headed and brave men to stand and lead and let those who suffer from spiritual and emotional immaturity to pause and catch their breath.

The consciousness of this world is shifting, there is no doubt. The question is no longer whether the world is shifting but rather what is the capacity that you will contribute to its transforming bend? What role will you play as the planet heals from its wars of competition, scarcity and the need to be proven right? As we adjust to the abundance of cooperation, creativity and sustainability, what capacity will you fill? Will you allow yourself to surrender your life to a calling that like distant noise in the night won't let you sleep? Can you live a life led by a purpose far greater than paying bills and checking off "to-do lists" while your inner principles are the very thing you will never negotiate? Do you have the courage to step into the fire of self-inquiry and let it burn you to your roots, shake you to your very core as it eliminates and strips away everything that you are not? And can you lay down the sword you picked up as a boy to slay others that criticize and disagree with you and turn that weapon on the very limiting beliefs that keep you from loving yourself, your woman and the world to their maximum and deserved capacity?

This is a call to you to live a life from the core of your being, unmoved by the critics of the world outside you. It is invitation to recapture the wildness of your heart and live as though freedom were your very next breath. If you have the courage to answer the call, the earnestness to seek a new way within and forgive the past and leave it where it belongs, the willingness to step into the fire and lay down the sword that has been cutting you for years, and the heart that has been yearning to live a life of value, freedom and purpose, then let us answer that call. Let us begin the most critical journey and let us discover that answer, together.

3 Damaging Words

This journey together is about evolution, ascension and creating an entirely new reality for us all to live in. Together we will explore limitations and what lies in emerging beyond them. We'll examine social norms that have been digested for decades even though they are becoming a poisonous paradigm. And we will also inquire about the self-imposed walls that we construct ourselves and live within as though there is no escape as we become resigned to our own trappings. One of the greatest bricks that makes up our own mental and emotional prison is a simple and overly accepted term, "Be a man."

The words or language to the phrase above have no intrinsic harm or by any means pose as a malicious threat from the speaker or the listener. But the insidious damage that they can cause over time can bring monumental confusion. There is nothing wrong with being a man and together we will overcome the shame of toxic masculinity. The problem and confusion lies in the question of what actually is "a man?" I have had countless amounts of men come to me for coaching at the point in which their relationships or marriages are truly suffering. Often times after I ask them what they feel the issue is and many reply, "My woman keeps telling me I need to be a man." To which they almost automatically reply, "I thought I was; I work hard, I keep it together, I do what I thought men do. But I guess, in all honesty, I really don't know what being a man is."

Without any clear definition of what it is to "be a man" the young men receiving this command are left to default to social norms;

the John Wayne archetype, hide your emotions, star athlete, always have the answer, never admit when you are afraid and certainly never let people see you sweat. Hearing that you need to be a man is actually setting you up for failure as it points to being an impossible figure. It would be as absurd as hearing "be successful without making any mistakes along the way." The very underpinnings of the statement point to an impossible standard that have men charge forward destructively, leaving a wake of collateral damage in their path of life and relationships and have no access to emotion or heart centered spaces within themselves. Or, the sentiment leaves men paralyzed with fear, afraid of making mistakes, decisions and trusting themselves because messing it up isn't what men do and "failure is not an option." These two outcomes are far from ideal and leave men either emotionally cut off from their hearts or overly sensitive to criticism and resigned to lives of doubt and over-analysis. Far from ideal options men are faced with an "either/or" scenario of being emotionally distant or being paralyzed by fear of failure. Neither is appealing but in our current cultural context a man is forced to choose one or the other.

There is no denying that men and women face challenges in our current culture. They are equal although they are distinct. Women are plagued with matching impossible standards of beauty and youth that do not befall men. Women have been conditioned to think their value is in how they look, how they love, and that self-worth is an external game. As men we have been taught that our worth and value is more related to how we perform, what we earn and that we are defined by our success and accomplishments. Living a life of external accumulations that pose as a promise will fill the void within our hearts that we were required to turn off to generate our earnings. Both unconscious conditionings of men and women are harmful and deteriorate our happiness and vitality. Both leave us empty and depleted and left searching in a world that will never deliver on such a promise.

There is an old Native American wisdom that says "the longest journey a man can make is only fourteen inches, the journey from his head to his heart." As we evolve the conversation of what it is to be a man we open options for men to once again, or perhaps for the first time, begin to connect with our emotional body. The goal is to not separate the head and the heart but to integrate them so as to create a balance of logic and passion, of reason as well as inspiration. One of the most damaging ingredients to the health of men is suppressed emotion; having no outlet to make sense of navigating what it is that we feel while having no language to put emotion to words and therefore running from it and from the fear of discomfort.

Allowing men to feel and even trust that we can handle our emotional state to fuel us shifts the conversation of masculinity from "don't feel your feelings" to "use them." Use them to fuel you, to open you up, to inspire you, to have you take risks and fall flat on your face for most of them and actually have the ability to hit the ground laughing. Use your feelings to propel you rather than para-lyze you; to have the ability to speak from your heart and use your logic to organize your inner world so that you can communicate like an effective leader.

All this points to a new definition of a man. A New Man Emerging. The term "be a man" causes no harm when what we are pointing to is a man of honor, of wisdom, of patience, compassion and love. This is a man willing to step into a fire of self-inquiry and burn away heartache, guilt and inner doubt, then to emerge from the fire loving, open, forgiving, fueled by inner freedom to forge ahead a life of purpose and fulfillment. If we are to use the term, "be a man," let us be that kind of man; a man that shows respect to his world and his woman or partner, a man that puts his honor and principles as the framework of his life, a man that holds his purpose dear to his heart and never negotiates it. He is a man that is willing to hear the harsh criticism of the world and yet goes on living his mission without distraction from the naysayers of possibility.

If we are to "man up" and "be a man" let us define the man we are aiming at and be proud of where we are pointing ourselves and the generations of men to follow. Let us leave a map that allows them to navigate the world through their own inner values and principles. Let us be the protectors of our earth and women so that feminine beauty and natural beauty are encouraged to flourish. Let us, together, make the journey from head to heart and live as integrated beings of peace and possibility. Let us point our aim towards this standard, this ascension, this new way of operating in the world and with this, let us "be a man."

NME Exercise:

Get quiet by closing your eyes and taking a few deep breaths. Notice your mind and your body as you breathe. Get yourself relaxed and then, from a place of non-judgment, begin to recall the moments in your past when you were told to "be a man" or told that you weren't being "man enough." Remember those moments but more importantly connect to thoughts, feelings and sensations that you experienced at that time. After connecting with those experiences, write down the conclusions that you drew from those experiences of your life. Connect to the assumptions and limiting beliefs that you concluded and how those have shaped your current worldview of what a man is today.

Tapping into the Eternal

"To fear death, gentlemen, is no other than to think oneself wise
when one is not, to think one knows what one does not know. No
one knows whether death may not be the greatest of all blessings for a
man, yet men fear it as if they knew that it is the greatest of evils."

— Socrates

Let us fast forward to the end: one day you are going to die. It is a fate that is written for us all. The last time I checked, the mortality rate is still at 100%. In the West, we are taught to fear death, delay it, deny it as though it will never happen or procrastinate it the best we can. By not knowing what comes next it has us proceed cautiously as though there was a way to control the inevitable by getting lost in our daily tasks and checking off boxes of what makes up a life well lived; school, job, girl, house, so on and so on. But at the deepest part of your spirit will that be enough for you? Will you settle for the conformity and mediocrity that surrounds you and drips like a slow daily poison or will you wake up to the shackles that have imprisoned you by your own limited thinking? Will you make of this life a daring and bold adventure that calls to you in the depths of your heart and soul or will you allow it to fade like a whisper in the night?

My intention for this book is not to prove the afterlife or what comes next. I will let you and your beliefs and inner explorations conclude that for yourself. My aim is to presence anything that ignites the purpose deep within you to make its way to the foreground of your heart, your mind and your consciousness. My invitation to you regarding your own death is to re-frame it, to keep it close and to contemplate it as a gift that gives meaning to life. The tragedy in life is not that we die; it is that we live as though we never will. We delay our deepest heart's desires for the immediate comfort of procrastination and we assume that inspirations unfed and unattended to will make their way back to our table. They won't. Our inspirations will find another table to dine at where the bread rises to the passions of flames that are committed to feeding it. The moments of life pass, if you miss it, you miss it. It's gone.

> *I imagine death so much it feels more like a memory"*
> — Lin-Manuel Miranda

Imagine a rose that never dies. A flame that never goes out. A song that never ends. It is the very limitation and scarcity of form that gives these poetries meaning. As we begin to surrender to the inevitability of one day ceasing in this form, we can then live with the same declaration that because we will one day pass on, that our life has a value, a meaning and a purpose perhaps yet undiscovered. By opening ourselves up to the shedding of this body we can begin a new exploration of being present to the part of us that doesn't die, that simply transforms, the part of us that is eternal. I can honestly say that although my father is gone my communication with him has not ceased. He lives in my memory, continues to guide my decisions and actions and whispers to me in the wind along with all my ancestors.

Let me be clear, I am not suggesting that you go out and seek your death. That would be careless and reckless and would do no good in defining why you are here. Rather, I am proposing that by knowing our fate, we can be free to live with a sense of deliberateness that has us create urgency and value in our lives. Your tombstone is certain, what is written on it is still up to you. In this, you become the generator of your fate. Living a life beyond "that's the just the way it is" and rather extracting purpose and presence to the eternal moment in front of you.

There is a great paradox to this life. All human beings have the need to be significant; that in this world of 7 billion people there is and must be something unique about me, which I play a part somehow, and there is a reason and purpose to my existence. We crave the knowledge of knowing that I am not an accident but rather a deliberate creation that was thought out by an intelligence far greater than myself. So we design lives to achieve, to stand out, and to accomplish goals that will ultimately leave a mark on infinity. And while we seek this life of significance, when we look from nature's perspective, we are intensely reminded that our place in the grand scheme of it all is tiny, insignificant and borderline irrelevant and that nature moves on despite our place; that the age of the universe is ungraspable to our limited minds. When we stand next to mountains and oceans we realize we are a tiny drop of water in an infinite ocean of discovery, movement, possibility and vastness. To stand in the middle, between the balance of the two, significance and insignificance, to know that simultaneously we are everything and nothing at the same time, at first may feel overwhelming. However, by exploring this paradox we can create a tremendous amount of freedom for ourselves. We can play our lives all out while resting in the knowing that nature operates in our growing favor.

There is place within you, that is still, quiet, unmoving, like the depths of the ocean. On the surface there could be weather raging, waves that have all the elements of chaos and even destruction. But below the surface, if you are willing to travel deep enough, there is a stillness that is unmoved by the surface's storm. Deep below there is a calm, a tranquility that is uninterested in the surface and is completely content with its deep nature. The same place lives within you. Below the surface of the everyday storms or even monotony of daily life, there is a place that dwells in you that is eternal, unchanging and unmovable. Can you tap into it? Can you live from this space that has you bring peace and calm to all your endeavors? As you explore this home within you, you will have the ability to lead your life from a place of presence, aliveness and let it lead you. Your woman and your world will be safe to relax in your presence and trust that you are unmovable; not rigid in your mind, but rather unwilling to bend in relationship with your principles and life's purpose.

The new emerging man seeks to make peace with his death. To befriend it and create a relationship of permission and agreements. As though they agreed on "if you, death, do not take me today, that is another day to give my gifts, live with purpose and love from the depth of my heart." At this, perhaps secretly, death smiles. Each day he ignores your door is another day of loving, of giving, of witnessing the magic that is within you and this world. To see it and experience it is solely up to you.

If you died today, would you be satisfied? Have you given this life everything that your Creator has asked of you to give? Have you explored the deepest levels of your being that would have you excited and surrendered to the next mysterious phase? Have you loved from the rooms of your heart that took years of suffering and prying to open? And have you lived with a sense of vision that had every step you took be deliberate, focused and purposeful. If the answer is no, that is honest. Now is the time to recapture the mystery within you that would have this life be an infinite wonder, a playground to your imagination and a platform for you to deliver your greatest purpose.

NME Exercise:

Lie down, close your eyes and take a few deep breaths. Imagine you are at your own funeral. Who is there? Who is not there? Who didn't come because of grudges or lost connection? What is the weather like? Who speaks about you? What do they say or not say?

As you go through this process, notice if you are satisfied because you are living congruently to your purpose or notice if you are perturbed with regret due to your life being out of alignment with what you desire. Notice any shifts and changes you can begin to make in your life and incorporate them immediately.

THE MYTH OF "ONE DAY"

"One day" is not coming. Many men have bought the myth that one day "my life will get easier, I'll figure it all out, my woman will understand me, I will finally get it all 'done." My apologies if I disappoint you, but one day is not coming. Life is not going to get easier, you are not going to figure it all out and it's certainly not your woman's job to get you and understand you if you yourself aren't willing to throw yourself into a fire of self-inquiry that would have her yearn to explore the nature of existence with you.

Most men have resigned themselves to lives of tasks, deadlines, project approvals and checklists. They were told to work hard, save enough and color inside the lines with a promise that "one day" they will get to enjoy the fruits of their labor. Meanwhile, the spirit in them, the boy inside, the longing, the fire of creativity and wonder slowly fades to a low whisper or to a flicker of an ash before it finally goes out.

A man would only make this trade with the promise that one day it would all be worth it. And yet, there is no guarantee. The New Man Emerging does not compromise his authenticity, aliveness, spontaneity and purpose to gamble on a hope that has left most men before him emotionally bankrupt; a promise that guarantees the diminishing of his wild spirit through conformity and requests of him in return his dreams and desires, his personal power and his uniqueness and creativity.

Your death is coming; "one day" is not. To delay your life's purpose and live a life of "quiet desperation" as Thoreau stated it is to forget the magic that this life and moment contain. The same is true if you deny the gift that you are and the talent that you have been given to contribute to a world that so desperately requests it of you now. Most men have been content with pressing the snooze button of their lives with a desperate hope that one day it will all be worth it and that it will all work out. Your power lies in this moment. Here. Now.

If your day-to-day tasks and processes don't align with your greater purpose in life, begin now, letting them go. Have the courage to risk a life of conformity for the possibility of ultimate freedom. This is your promise from your Creator: that you live a life that you are proud of, that fuels your creativity and love and that the world is left better because you were here. Not simply because you existed; but rather, because you chose to live a life that had meaning, purpose and an urgency that was unwilling to wait, to compromise and to put your fate in anyone's hands but your own.

When a man lives for "one day" he begins to put all his power in outcomes. Naturally, being results driven creatures we will tend to believe that the outcome is what has power, that the result is what determines our inner state and our happiness. When he believes that the promise of achievement will hold some ultimate pinnacle of life and after accomplished a man will now kick back, rest and be finished. So, in this present moment a man will bare down, white knuckle it, trudge through life hoping to reach a summit of life rather than allow the present moment and journey to shape him along the way. Here's the secret: it never ends. Life will always be unfolding and there is no proverbial summit. There is no final destination that will have you completely relaxed and surrendered and clear to the meaning of your life. The meaning is "in" your life; the meaning and presence that you are giving it along the way. It is cliché but adamantly true, it is the journey that shapes us. One of my mentors used to say that on the road to self-realization, we chop wood and carry water. During self-realization we no longer chop wood and carry water.

After self-realization we chop wood and carry water. The ebb and flow of life and its gifts and challenges never ends. Stop thinking it will.

This points us to a valuable perspective, "What" you are striving for is not as important as "why." Why strive? What is the innate knowing in you that knows there is something more to the day than wake up, work and repeat? If your hope is that the accomplishment of some goal will leave you eternally happy, then you are sacrificing your power and will miss the magic of this moment. The journey that calls forth your presence, power, gifts, talents and creativities will keep you alive as opposed to simply existing for "one day." What is great enough for you that you would give yourself over to it and allow the journey of becoming to shape you rather than the journey of achieving? What would be so large that you would walk into the fire and allow it to burn away all your comparing, waiting and delaying the gift that you are in this moment? What are you pretending not to know about how powerful you are and what you were put on this earth to do?

Oh me! Oh life! of the questions of these recurring,
Of the endless trains of the faithless, of cities fill'd with the foolish,
...
Of the poor results of all, of the plodding and sor-
did crowds I see around me,
Of the empty and useless years of the rest, with the rest me intertwined,
The question, O me! so sad, recurring—What
good amid these, O me, O life?

Answer.
That you are here—that life exists and identity,
That the powerful play goes on, and you may contribute a verse.
— Walt Whitman

"That the powerful play goes on and that you may contribute a verse." My promise to you is that there is a verse in you, far greater than even you have imagined. That there is a poetry to your life that longs to be written. A song yearning to be sung. And a unique fire in you that craves the oxygen that only you your breath can feed. What will your verse be? What will be made better because you lived? What is the poem inside you that you will allow the hands of your life to write?

QUESTION #1

I spend time daily contemplating my life as well as my death. Determined to give all that I have, I am fueled by a sense of urgency that propels me forward; a purpose that moves me past my comfort zone and creates a sense of gratitude and wonder for the present moment. When life gets hectic, from time to time I pause, look up at the sky and remember how magnificent the world is in which I live.

Through years of these contemplations I have often wondered what would be on the other side of my passing. If the Great Spirit were to welcome me in heaven what would be the questions asked of me? Over the years, I have come up with two questions... The first I will share with you now.

When I die I believe God will ask me this... "How well did you tend to that unique fire that I put in your heart?"

I live my life by this question. I don't believe that God, The Great Mystery, cares how much money I've made or the things I've accumulated, how many trophies and accolades I've earned, how many women's hearts I broke or what the title of my job was before I hung it up. All these things we tend to chase on earth seem insignificant in the face of what we can or cannot take with us when we die. To shift and live a life where my gifts are my assets and what I contribute is my currency has developed a sense of purpose and freedom that I have never experienced while working for someone else's dream of competing and keeping up with the status quo.

That verse, that fire in you, is unique to you. There are particular gifts that have been endowed to as you walk this earth. Do you know what they are? Do you utilize and tend to them on a daily basis that would have you live a life of purpose and meaning? However great or small you conclude those gifts to be, they are yours to steward, cultivate or ignore. Look to your passions and the experiences that light you up and create a sense of wonder, gratitude and joy. That is the very heart of who you are and one of the most profound ways that your spirit communicates with you.

If you are to ignore those communications and messages that is entirely your right. But to follow them, to tend to them and feed them so that they become the driving force in your life is to live from a deeper place. It is a place that has everything you do and commit to become alive with meaning and deliberateness. Human consciousness has forever been drawn toward freedom; to experience full self-expression, to love unabashed and to live unapologetically. That fire is within each one of us and it invites us all, though it's the extraordinary ones that have the courage to accept its call.

For some of us that fire has dwindled. But the promise is that it has not been snuffed out completely. Years of pandering, ignoring and compromising our inner passions and principles begin to wear down the framework of fulfillment that yearns to grow within the heart of a man. The New Man Emerging does not wait for the fire within him to grow so that it eventually becomes a light to the outside world. Rather, he feeds it, nurtures it with the fuel of his willingness to take risks, to fail, to own his gifts and contribute them to the platform that he chooses or is called to in life.

The wealthiest place in the world is probably not far from where you live. If you want to experience it, put down this book and go to your local cemetery. It is loaded with un-manifested dreams, buried with solutions and possibilities and peppered with lives that never met their true potential. Run by fear rather than freedom the majority of lives in a cemetery were motivated by other people's approval and waited for society to give them the green light and go-ahead to live a life they truly imagined. Rather than fuel their inner fire with love, freedom, boldness and aliveness they ran their lives by "what if" and "if only." Mentally limiting themselves, they were not truly free to express their inner most creativities and desires but instead they allowed their fear to enter their home until it finally became their host.

If you are waiting for the fire to grow on its own while suffocating it with distractions and procrastinations, then the world, your woman and your life are being done a disservice. The world and your life owe you nothing. You are the one that owes something to your life and the world. Now is the time, more than ever, to fuel the fire within you so that it can be a beacon of a passionate, purposeful and committed life.

If you haven't experienced that fire in a long time, or perhaps even ever, that is okay, the time is still right. Begin today. Do something today, however great or small, that expands your heart and reminds you of what it is to be alive. Do something that scares you, something you have put off doing for years, take the risk and live into it, knowing that your passion and fortitude will see you through. If you don't, it is another douse of water on the fire that aches in you rather than feeding it the oxygen it so desperately deserves.

NME Exercise:

Begin to make a list of all the things you have always said you wanted to do or experience. Determine how long you have wanted to do it and the actions (or lack thereof) you have taken to make it happen. Chose one thing from the list and take an immediate action on it within 24 hours of doing this exercise.

OUR GREATEST POISON

As we awaken, we must look within ourselves to see the barriers that we have imposed on our lives. We must, with great courage and fortitude, slay the dragons of our own inner being, thus allowing us to be open, engaged in life and free to express our deepest desires and wisdom. Before designing a new life and world we must rid ourselves of the greatest toxic poison that we have continued to ingest over our lives: fear.

The human body has not changed much over the last 10,000 years. Physiologically we are predominantly the same as our ancestors. Their fear kept them alive because it was a natural instinct that warned them against predators and got them to safety. For our ancient relatives, danger was a matter of life and death. Our bodies today, react very similar to the way they did thousands of years ago to danger and stress; a flood of adrenaline, a spike of cortisol stress hormone, making us bigger, stronger and faster for a brief amount of time until we could rest in safety.

Our bodies may not have changed much, but our everyday lives have. We have culturally designed lives of comfort as to have no need to deal with life threating elements and we don't flee from giant predators and big cats in our daily routine. And yet the fear response in us is just the same. Although instead of fighting or fleeing physical beasts, we now are directed inward to the predators of our own mind.

The dragons we are designed to fight today are our own doubt, worry, insecurities and seeming lack of control of our destiny and future. We treat these internal concepts as though they were tangible threats to our existence. We have replaced dangerous creatures with the masks and dogmas of what it means to be successful and the fear of what would happen if we fall short of that imaginary standard.

Fear of failing or even the fear of success has many men today paralyzed by their own fictitious imaginings and has cut off the access to their greatest attributes and allies of courage, fortitude, vulnerability and passion. To the future belongs the bold; those who are willing to see where fear has a strong hold on them and possess the willingness to release it into the fire.

It is fear that has us delay, wait and withhold our greatest contributions to the world. Fear has us hide behind masks and not reveal our true authentic selves. We have concluded that to not risk being rejected is a safer passage than living a life full out, with the possibility and high probability of stumbling along the way and that it is better to live a life of safety and conformity than to stand out and speak up when voices go unheard. We imagine the risks to be too great but often never examine the opposite. Rarely do we reflect on the prices that we pay by living within those comfort zones only to find how truly uncomfortable our comfort zone is. The prices we pay of emotion suppression and inner freedom just to get a small dose of approval and social acceptance As well as the price of joy to live a life of deep and meaningful expression that has us congruent with our deepest life purpose.

Fear, like evil, rarely announces itself. It is insidious. It makes its way into our lives not through heavy toxic doses, but rather through slow drips that over time make the spirit sick with nothing truly to point at as the ultimate culprit. Fear strangles us one compromise at a time. It finds room in our complacent thinking that has one small procrastination and delay convince us that there will always be "another day" to tackle our life's greatest work. Comfort by comfort, compromise by compromise, giving in to our fear has us lost on our pathway to greatness and fulfillment.

It is fear that has had us do the most heinous things to our fellow man and it is fear that has made itself far too familiar in our homes. As long as fear dines at your table, do not wonder why the bread hasn't risen or why the wine doesn't taste as sweet. The New Man Emerging sees that his fear was welcomed and even placed there by him and it is his responsibility and his alone to evict it from his table and from his thinking. Freedom is his ultimate goal. Outwardly, it is that all men be free from oppression and social institutions that seek otherwise. And even greater is his drive to be free of the oppressor that he has placed on himself through his own inner critic, his skepticism and his limiting beliefs. He is committed to rewriting the absurd story that he has created that somehow it could actually be dangerous to truly love. Free from this poison, he is free to live a life unencumbered, of true design of love and creativity, not needing society or life's permission or approval.

All great men have fear, but for average men, fear has them. Fear, in small doses, reminds us that we are alive. It hints at us to wake up and remember that life and happiness are not guaranteed. But when it stays for too long we begin to grow use to its company. Eventually it owns us through paralyzing us. The New Man Emerging does not wait for the fear to go away. He creates a new relationship with it. Rather than be paralyzed by its grip, he uses it to create urgency to leave nothing undone. He breathes and connects with the moment and evicts the limiting thoughts and beliefs that would have the average man stop. "It's too hard," "I don't have what it takes," "What if I fail?" And rather than be restrained by his beliefs, he reshapes them to work for him rather than against him. This takes discipline and time. Fortunately, mastery is his goal. Rather than let his limiting beliefs cripple him, he examines them, brick by brick and questions and challenges them to their very core. Limitations, when truly examined, never stand the test of time.

Our fearful beliefs are exactly that, beliefs. They are not truths. No matter how many times you have tried to prove them to be. No matter how many times you have reminded yourself how hard it will be or how painful it will be if you fail. Your beliefs are superstitions at best. As you examine them and test them against your reality and ultimate experience you will begin to find that they don't hold up.

That they are constructed on faulty inner soil and that the narrative you tell yourself about your greatness has a far stronger footing.

NME Exercise:

Question your fear. For years we live as though our assumed fears are true. They trap us. One of our greatest allies to handling our fear is to challenge them. Begin to become aware of your thinking. Notice when fear comes in. Get to the core of the belief system so that you can identify the narrative that you listen to. Your beliefs may include "I am not enough", "I don't have what it takes" and "I don't deserve it or I'm not worth it." Get to the heart of it. Then simply ask yourself if that is true and if it serves you. True means that you can prove it without a doubt. Serves you means that it brings you closer to the life you desire. Once you answer both questions take an action on something that actually supports your growth in that moment. Do it right then and there. Practice this over and over again and watch what begins to happen to the ground those beliefs try to stand on.

Your Comfort Zone is Elastic

Human beings, especially men, are not a "fixed reality." We are not confined to one way of operating in time and space. "There's nothing I can do about it," "it's just the way it is," I am who I am and can't change" and on and on. We live as though we are constricted, restrained and confined to the very limits and labels that we self-impose and even self-inflict upon ourselves. We are not fixed in time with limited movement, and most importantly, neither is our comfort zone.

Thoreau once said "most men lead lives of quiet desperation." Though he said that in the 1800's this statement rings as true today as ever. The image of men silently screaming to break free from mental prisons is poignant and heartbreaking. But when truly examined we can see that we are the ones that locked the doors to our hearts and minds and we are the ones that hold the key. The fear of breaking free of our comfort zones is what has us trapped far more than any authority, doctrine or class. We have created limitations that over time seem as though the walls are solidified, that we are trapped in dead end jobs, unfulfilled relationships and dreams that will never make it through the night and see the light of day.

Your fear is natural. It reminds you of the mental limits that you have developed and placed on yourself. You have determined that inside those limits you are safe and that outside those boundaries it is scary and uncomfortable. Your fear determines the line. However, when truly examined you can see that all of your growth takes place on the other side of that limit and that your comfort zone is, oddly enough, incredibly uncomfortable.

Living a life of purpose will be uncomfortable. Discomfort is the price of admission for living a life of purpose and meaning. It will have you stand out when it seems far safer to blend in. It will have you speak up when you see silence all around you and it will require of you to act even when fear has placed its grip on you. The New Man Emerging does not wait for the fear to go away, he doesn't wait for the waters to calm or things to all be perfect. Instead, he forms a new relationship with fear. He doesn't try to ignore or suppress it or analyze it away. He acts with clarity, moves forward from a place of courage while he welcomes his fear to challenge him and remind him of his self-imposed limits. Only so that he now has the opportunity to grow past them.

Many men spend their entire lives waiting for the fear to dissolve, dissipate or go away; only to spend their whole lives waiting. Fear doesn't go away because you are the one that put it there! No amount of over analysis is going to have it disappear. You cannot think your way out of your fear because you are the one that is dreaming it up. A knife can cut 1,000 things but it can never cut itself. Neither will your logic solve your fear, your mind dreamt it up, only your heart can conquer it.

Courage is not the absence of fear, quite the contrary. Courage is the ability to do something that frightens you; to feel it, face it, and move forward anyway. Fear, like death, can be one of your greatest allies when used to propel you rather than paralyze you. Too often men seek courage in their mind, find the root cause of it and slay it so that the fear goes away. Though valuable to recognize patterns and see where habits stem from, moving forward puts a man's focus on the future, the unknown; A place where there is no database of research to reference because it has not happened yet. Stepping into this unknown requires courage, presence and willing to be open to victory and defeat and have the humility to treat them both equally, knowing that there is growth and awakening in both. Navigating the unknown future with reason only is limiting. As a man makes his heart pure, a clear mind will certainly follow.

Luckily, the walls of our comfort zone are not cemented but rather they are elastic. They stretch when expanded. A rubber band when pulled never returns to its original form, although it seems that way to the eye. Same with you; when you are stretched, you grow, when you stay stagnant you slowly die. Stagnation is death. By remaining unwilling to grow past your perceived limits you will over exercise your logical certainties while allowing your heart, passions and inner freedoms to become atrophied.

To be clear, this doesn't suggest that you pretend you have no limits and recklessly barrel through your life. This will have you leaving collateral damage in the wake of your life and will eventually require you to do massive cleanup in your relationships from your unconsciousness. To the other extreme, if you find yourself hiding, delaying and procrastinating living the life you truly desire because you imagine the walls of your comfort zone too daunting or strenuous to climb that they have you back away and spend your life waiting for the right moment that will guarantee painlessness, then you are deluding yourself.

Rather, what I am suggesting is to find the edge of your comfort zone and instead of plowing past it with some unsustainable energy or shrinking from it and letting it rule your life, I suggest you simply lean on it. Day after day. Push by push, move it. Do something each day that contributes to the stretching of your comfort zone, something that scares you, challenges you so that over time you can look back and assess how far you have come from where you started. This is the way to grow and become conscious of the life you truly want to live.

At my father's funeral I gave a eulogy about the lessons that he taught me. When he was diagnosed with pancreatic cancer, a diagnosis that typically is a few months or a year to live at best, he taught me his final lesson: When life puts a mountain in front of you that you cannot climb nor get around, you simply lean on it, and move it. Day by day, push by push, inch by inch. That was his lesson to me. With that, my father moved the mountain of pancreatic cancer for 8 years.

The fear is not going anywhere. It will grow with you as you grow. We are not fixed in time but rather we are an ever-evolving possibility that is congruent with the inner states that we choose. And as you choose to move and stretch so too will your courage. As you evolve into the possibility that you are, your comfort zone will stretch with you, reminding you of how far you have come and the limits you continue to place on yourself so that you can dive deeper into the challenge and celebration of being human. And you will then begin to experience what it is to live with an open heart led by purpose and fulfillment and to live a life that is generated by your vision instead of your fear.

Our Current Epidemic

Whether we have turned off our hearts to charge through life toward results or we have become so overly analytical that we are afraid to make any step toward advancement because we are too critical of ourselves or too sensitive to others' feedback, the result of either is a half-lived life. With a head down racing through life to the next thing or holding back inspirations for fear of embarrassment or failure, we miss life. We literally miss it. Seasons come and go, our children grow up and we wonder where time went and our life's dreams become distant memories. We wonder where it all went. We settle for fleeting glimpses of peace, sprinkled moments of happiness and resign ourselves to being at the mercy of fate rather than its author. The life half-lived is an epidemic.

In battle, knowing your true enemy is good fortune. When the enemy is within, danger is always present. Our current epidemic is one from within. We must presence it and highlight it so as to know what it is, how it operates and what it takes from us. A life half lived is a life de-valued. We must be vigilant of it so we can know where it grows and how to cut it out from its roots. Like evil, this epidemic doesn't announce itself. It creeps in slowly, insidiously and makes its way into your heart and mind by only whispering. Though let us not forget that a forest fire can start from a single ember or that a revolution can spring from one promising idea. The half-lived life is patient; it doesn't need all its fortunes at once but rather prefers to spread them out over the course of your life. Knowing this, we can eliminate it, stunt its growth and support others along their journey toward fulfillment. To cure the epidemic we must starve out its food supply. What the half-lived life feeds upon is *compromise of spirit* and *complacency of thinking.*

Compromise of Spirit

The fire inside you is not going to extinguish, so it's far better that you feed it. Buried under delay and doubt we think we can run from it, delay it until life is comfortable and the setting is right. All the while it waits. The fire inside you longs to live, to experience itself in full flame but is often snuffed out by limiting beliefs of "not now" and suffocated by "what if" scenarios of the mind. For every compromise we make on our life's purpose and goals, we grow further and further away from our vitality and lose the power of our own aliveness. We push our inspirations away thinking they will come again or worse yet defeat ourselves by thinking "who am I to be great?" As Marianne Williamson perfectly put it…

> *"Our deepest fear is not that we are inadequate. Our deepest fear is that we are powerful beyond measure. It is our light, not our darkness that most frightens us. We ask ourselves, 'who am I to be brilliant, gorgeous, talented, fabulous?' Actually, who are you not to be?"*

Conformity and darkness have become a norm. We are bombarded by naysayers and countless reasons to play it safe in our lives. We hear overwhelmingly convincing arguments of why it is foolish and childish to chase dreams and actually go for a life worth living. We believe that somehow it is mature to give up heartfelt inspirations and become reasonable and realistic while secretly celebrating the people that actually "went for it" in life as we convince ourselves that no fate could ever bless us the same way.

This conversation is a poison and it is the one that needs to be dealt with immediately so that it can be healed and eliminated. A man's spirit needs to be fueled, inspired and cared for. Every time we engage in a conversation of doubt, every time we settle for less than magnificent and every time we believe a limiting belief of perceived smallness, we take up space in our soul that could otherwise be filled with contribution and greatness. We diminish the oxygen required to fuel the fire within and instead feed it to the demons of doubt, delay and isolation. Every time we compromise our vision, the thing that truly lights us up from within, we chip away at our esteem and worthiness. Compromise is patient, like a cancer it grows slowly, but is determined to feed off of the host.

It is time to stop compromising our lives. Time to stop waiting for conditions and circumstances to be right and comfortable or have all our outcomes guaranteed before we take action. It is time to live a life worth living; to begin today, to do, in however small a way, the very thing that lights you up from within. This is not a call to recklessness; on the contrary, it is a call to priority. What fuels you in life doesn't belong in the backseat of your heart and mind. It belongs in the foreground; as a guiding light of your very soul. It belongs as the true north of your inner compass that will have all your endeavors be meaningful and purposeful. Without it, you are simply existing, and hope will be your only friend.

Every time you compromise your heart's desire you send a message that you, your dreams and your passions, aren't worth the priority of your time, love and energy. You put yourself in the background of your own existence and remain confused and lost as to why life isn't fulfilling and electric. Every time you sell out on what you know would light up your spirit and set your soul on fire for the safer road, for the sake of "being reasonable", you chip away at your self-esteem and personal power.

Living a life of "what if" works both ways. As we look forward, we let fear stand in our way and say, "what if it doesn't work out? What if I fail? What if I don't have what it takes?" We allow 'what if' to paralyze us. And yet it works the opposite way as well. Looking back on our lives we will also say with immense regret, "What if I went for it and worked out? What if I had it happen, what if I messed it up but learned from it, what if I actually had what it took?" Unfortunately, at that point, there will be no answers, it will be too late and regret is all you get. As John Greenleaf Whittier wrote; "For all sad words of tongue and pen, the saddest are these, 'it might have been.'"

For letting fear stop us, we join the masses in the cemeteries of what could have been. We bury our hopes, our dreams, our solutions and insights. We get a false sense of safety by playing it small. We get a sense of staying within our comfort zone and not needing to access confidence and power by actually standing out. But we also pay the price of giving up freedom, fulfillment and self-expression. We lose out on the adventure of life and seek to make the best out of monotony and boredom. We live lives half expressed, wondering what could have been more and ignore the deep callings of our soul. We default to band aiding our wounds rather than committing to the willingness that deep healing requires. Masking our true selves with appearances, we become unwilling to uproot the parts of our lives that we know aren't working and instead settle for facades and assumed identities. All the while, the spirit in us is crying out, longing for expression, dying to be loved and once again feel the magnificence of what life can offer.

We, as men, must cease listening to the compromising voice inside our heads. It is false, untrue and dangerous. The good news is that it isn't real. It was put there early in our lives and can be eradicated. We are not broken, we can be healed and we have all that it takes to live lives of freedom, discipline, love and connection. It takes discipline and commitment to overcome the false and limiting beliefs that we have purchased over our lives. Begin today by buying them no longer. Like an old door-to-door salesman that used to knock on our entrances, apologize and simply ask them to be on their way. For every limiting belief including "You don't have what it takes," "You are unworthy," "Who are you to be great?", simply acknowledge them and ask them to depart from your doorway. You have purchased them long enough and the return on your investment has not sufficed.

It is time for a new possibility. One that leaves you open and free to explore the depths of this life and all it has to offer you. This is the sale you get to purchase; this is the investment that yields the greatest returns; not solely for you, but also for your family, your community and the world. You, living a life of freedom and passion is not only what the world needs, it's what it deserves.

We must let go of the pains of yesterday to truly experience the magic of this moment now. It is our right to reclaim our freedom from the insidious compromises of our past. It is now time to discipline our inner world so that fear and false beliefs are no longer louder than our ambitions and spiritual callings. Rather than feed fear with delay, distraction, procrastination and doubt it is now time to fuel our inner fire with passion and deliberateness.

The physical heart is sustained by blood. The spiritual heart is sustained by passion. Without passion the heart begins to atrophy and over time it will harden. With no visible scars, it will present itself as a life free of vitality and aliveness. I promise you there is more to your life than being one giant fire extinguisher to life's false emergencies. We must, as men, be willing to take risks, to be vulnerable and to leave ourselves open to opportunities that allow our hearts to break. And in so doing, exercise our most vital muscle with the aim to strengthen our capacity to love and live with purpose.

Complacency of Thinking

A long time ago... a man captured a wizard and made him grant a wish. He wished for a demon that would do as he asked. The wizard said that the man would have to keep the demon busy or it would grow and consume him. The man said "No problem!" and the wizard vanished. Then the demon appeared, about the size of a football. The man tried to keep the demon busy with tasks. He asked the demon to clean up his house. A minute later the demon returned and said, "It is done" and grew to the size of the man. He asked the demon to prepare a feast for his friends. The demon returned a few seconds later and said "It is done" and grew to the size of grizzly bear. He asked the demon to build a new house on the mountain. The demon returned a second later and said, "It is done" and grew to the size of his living room. As the tasks got more elaborate the demon simply returned sooner and said "It is done" and each time he returned he got larger and larger. The man went running out of his house, managed to outsmart the demon and finally came upon a wise man and told him of his predicament. The wise man said, "Give the demon this hair." and he handed the man a piece of curly hair. "Ask him to straighten it." The wise man disappeared and the demon appeared, larger and fiercer than ever. "What is your bidding?" The man cringed and handed him the hair and asked him to straighten it. The demon laughed. But as the demon found out, he couldn't straighten it. As he tried, he got smaller and smaller. Any time the man wanted the demon to do something; he asked for the hair back and asked the demon to do what he wanted. Then he handed the hair back to the demon. He lived happily ever after.

– Tom Brown, *The Quest*

The mind makes a far better servant than it does a master. In today's world we have grown to worship logic and reason and have glorified the mind into an over thinking, ever consuming entity that is never fully satiated and satisfied. Ultimately, in modern culture, the mind has become a misused tool.

While I was growing up, my father was a builder and a fine craftsman and I was always around power tools as a kid. Wisely, he would plug in the tool, turn it on, make a cut or whatever function was needed, then turn the tool off and unplug it. His craftsmanship was like no other and the things he built and created were remarkable. He knew how to use and operate his tools which included unplugging them they were not in use which kept me and my brothers safe around them.

The mind is much like these tools. When operating its function and turned on and off safely, it becomes one of the most powerful tools of creation. When plugged in, turned on and left unattended it becomes incredibly dangerous to all those around it.

An undisciplined mind is dangerous. When unattended, it becomes like a mismanaged tool that can cut others, and even more so, it's owner. As men, we tend to overuse or over-esteem the mind by thinking it is the only faculty to create from and thus delay or deny the heart. We tend to estimate that only reason is fact and that life can be figured out or put into some kind of formula or equation. Without the heart as the predominant source of creation the mind begins to consume a man and take over his state like the demon in the story. A man must learn to use his mind from a place of stillness, not to control it, but to use it as a way of consciously shaping his reality.

The mind thinks, it produces thoughts and puts words and language to experience. But to the degree that a man lives only from his mind, he will conceptualize life and miss his actual experiences. He will develop conclusions and live as though his thoughts and beliefs about himself or his life are final, written-in-stone truths rather than beliefs that can be challenged, shifted or even transformed. When the mind's concepts go unexamined, then life tends to go on automatic to a man's belief systems rather than his experience in the moment, here and now. Like a reflex, a man will filter the moment through his past and make conclusions based on yesterday, rather than truly experiencing this new moment.

Experiencing takes place now; belief systems are based on the past. The past isn't negative or something to run from, however, it is limited. It is limited to what has happened and then in the present moment we filter here and now through the window of yesterday. One of the greatest powers we have as human beings is the ability to un-collapse our concepts and beliefs from our experiences. The two are not the same. And in so doing, we now create an opportunity to be present in the moment, rather than default to a past belief, concept or the pain of yesterday.

If we let our mind go unchallenged and uninterrupted, we will constantly filter today through yesterday and limit our potential in the moment as well as our ability to generate a future of new possibility. If a man sees the potential of a passionate future of freedom and purpose but filters through a past lens of limited belief systems such as "I am not good enough," "I am unworthy, "I've tried before and failed," then his past belief system will shape his reality rather than his powerful inner world. He won't have access to his greatest faculty and agency of creation, which is his heart, because it will be clouded and suffocated by his limiting thinking of himself from the past.

As we quiet the mind through daily discipline and practice as well as access the courage to disrupt and interrupt old belief systems, we now have an opportunity generate a new future from a clear space of this moment. As men, we have been conditioned to try and figure out life, to make sense of it and to control it with our minds. Then, once we establish control, we can allow our hearts to safely participate in the moment. It won't work. The mind is powerful. Like a knife it can cut many things but it cannot cut itself. The mind will never "figure out" life because life isn't designed to be figured out, it is designed to be experienced. And experiences are not designed to make sense; they are designed to simply be experienced, in the moment.

NME Exercise:

Meditate. If you do not have a daily meditation practice start one immediately. Commit 10 mins each morning to closing your eyes and focusing on your breath. No music, no mantras, no distractions. Set a timer for 10 minutes and simply stay aware of your breathing until the alarm goes off. Do this each day, no compromise.

YOUR POWER IS YOUR PRESENCE

Your world and your woman deserve your presence. Your presence is the deep connection that you possess to the here and now. Your presence of self, moment, body, your thoughts and beliefs are the window and doorway into your inner state. This is beyond the ways that you act and behave; this is literally the ways that you are being. Courageous, honorable, honest, open, loving etc. are all ways of being that generate behaviors and actions thereafter.

Your presence is a gift to your woman (or spouse) and the world. To be present with each other we build up each others self esteem, significance and self worth. On the contrary, nothing harms your woman spirit or your children's self esteem faster than your emotional absence. By being conditioned to constantly seek for something more; some better future, some great accomplishment, some future mountaintop of life, we are consistently taking ourselves out of the present moment. We miss here and now. We are constantly dreaming of some other state than the one we are experiencing. Taught to suppress emotion, we tend to white knuckle our life as men, in pursuit of some promise that will lead to fulfillment while even if we achieve it, we are left emotionally unavailable and empty, seeking more and leaving emotional collateral damage to the ones we love along the way.

The irony is that the only way to influence and shape our future is by being conscious of the choices we are making here and now.

However, there is a distinction that needs to be highlighted here. Operating in the moment while generating a conscious aligned future congruent with your purpose leads to fulfillment and a meaningful life. Whereas, obsessing about a future because this present moment isn't enough, is unsatisfactory or uncomfortable, will ultimately lead to a life of struggle and resistance. Many of us find ourselves living a life of chasing an idea, a promise, and a misguided cultural paradigm with the hope that one day it will take us out of the nagging "unsatisfactory-ness" of here and now. In Buddhism, this concept of un-satisfactoriness is called "dhukka." Dhukka is that constant feeling that something is missing. Mistakenly, we then seek outside ourselves to fill that hole rather than cultivate the process of filling it in ourselves so that we no longer allow scarcity perspectives to shape our reality.

Presence is power. It is the choice to be here and now and from a place of acceptance rather than resistance. Presence generates new possibilities. Without presence, we don't have full access to choosing and cultivating our inner states. Without presence, we default to our automatic belief systems of the past and continue to produce results that we don't desire but unfortunately are just simply familiar. We lack critical thinking in this moment and we lack the discernment to connect and access what this very moment is calling forth. There is a tremendous amount of power in this process and the earlier statement. The challenge is this... can you be present enough to listen with your heart for the answer to one simple question...

"What is this moment calling forth from me?"

The commitment and dedication to constantly asking this question, and answering it with your actions, can change everything. This is the willingness to see that each moment has a gift and value and that your presence is the doorway to unlocking its secrets. When we are silent, present and actually listening, we can tap into the moment and bring to it what it calls for. There are moments when we are working, when we are with our children and spouses, that we are robotically acting the same, over and over. Without truly being present, we become automatic and lifeless and our energy and vitality become stripped and misguided. When we stop and choose to be present, we give life to our behaviors, actions and habits that renew richness to our lives and the current moment. This is not out of reach, but it does require a commitment to mastery over and over again.

Presence is a choice. This is where your power is. The moment of here and now is always here; your awareness of it and connection to it is entirely up to you. This is why choice is powerful. It requires your attention to be here and now which is not based on anything other than you simply choosing it. Your focus goes where you choose for it to go. This is power.

Right now, here in this moment, you can literally choose to bring your focus and attention to a part of your body like your legs, hands or between your eyes. You can stop in this moment and bring all of your attention to your breath and the rising and falling of your stomach and chest. You can also stop in this moment and bring all your attention and focus to your feelings and state here and now. And you can also bring all your awareness to your thinking and choose to think of certain thoughts of the past or even particular promises for the future. Notice that these are all generated initially by where you *choose* to put your awareness. That is why choice is so powerful as it relates to this present moment. From this perspective, we can actually say that we experience what we choose.

Now, most people are simply unaware or lack presence enough to see that by choosing, or defaulting to an automatic lack of presence, we are creating our experience in this moment. To the degree that we practice presence we can ultimately choose how we think, what we say and how we feel and act. This eliminates victimhood, the idea that life is happening to us rather than generated by us and how we choose to interpret life's events. This puts all the power back on us and in our hands. It eliminates excuses and circumstances that we disagree with and has us reshape ourselves to create the lives we truly desire.

The New Man Emerging is not a victim. He is the creator of his own fate and destiny and he understands that the greatest tool he has for transforming his life is to be present to the moment and the choices in front of him now.

At first this may feel overwhelming as you start out on this path of ownership through choosing. To look at life and see that it is up to you to generate it according to what you desire and that all the power rests in how you choose to live and act, may seem like a daunting task. But let us break it down so that is not only digestible but also empowering. Walk up to the ocean and witness its immensity and look for as far out on the horizon as you can until you see the ocean disappear. Take in how grand and endless it is, but then hold the water in your hands and look closely and understand that however vast the ocean is it is still is and always will be made up of tiny individual drops of water. Then look up and down the beach on which you stand and take in the endlessness of the shoreline. Reach down and pick up the beach in your hand and look closely and remember that the as vast as the beaches are they are and always will be made up of tiny individual grains of sand. And then look at your life both backwards and forwards, all the events of the past and hopes and dreams of the future. Take in how vast it is, and then remember that your life is and always will be made up of tiny, individual, moment-to-moment... choices. Always. And all the choices exist in this moment here and now. What we choose to experience and call forth in this moment over and over again will inevitably determine the outcomes of what we produce in our lives. The power is in our hands and our presence is required to connect to this moment here and now and focus our awareness on what it is that we choose to create in our lives.

SLAYING THE 3 "D"EMONS

At the end of the day, as well as at the end of our lives, we will inevitably see that we are the masters of our own fate or failure. It is wise to own this reality sooner rather than later. Though we have all been dealt different hands, we all share the same platform of possibility. Those that create extraordinary results are the ones that take full ownership of their fate. For the rest, they will be left with excuses and regrets and validation of being right about their self-imposed limitations. Hence, the wealthiest place in the world is the graveyard.

The New Man Emerging is the man that owns his own reality. He tills the plot of soil given to him in this life. Free of excuses and "if onlys" he is accountable for his actions and his story in this world. He doesn't blame the cards dealt to him but rather uses them to feed and fuel his mission in life. He looks back on his past and owns his actions, choices, decisions and results (or lack thereof) and never sends blame to anything or anyone. This is his life, he owns all of it.

Life has a way of handing us challenges. Just because we declare our lives to be great, to live our dreams and go for what we desire does not make us exempt from difficulties. In fact, there is a strong possibility that the greater the dream, the greater the challenge. The question is not whether or not we will be challenged as men, but how we choose to handle our adversities. Do we welcome obstacles or run from them? Do we rise to meet the challenge or do we shrink to find an easier path?

Standing in the way of your dreams are your demons. These demons were put in front of you to grow, to challenge you and to polish and hone your skills toward a life of mastery. And these demons were put there by you. This is why ownership of life is vital. Without this perspective we will constantly be victim to what lies in front of us. And we will automatically seek to run from it or judge it rather than learn from it and grow. Your dreams are on the other side of your demons, therefore you must learn to slay them.

Demon #1 - Doubt

"Doubt has killed more dreams than failure ever will."
— Suzy Kassem

As we rise in life, so do our challenges. They go hand-in-hand. Discomfort is the price we pay for living a deep and meaningful life. Challenges are inevitable as well as necessary. They stretch us and demand us to access creativity, humility, clarity, trust and confidence. Without challenges we would live average lives, free of incredible fire and passion and our spirits would atrophy like an unused muscle. Challenges are coming; they must be met with a greater force of love than the paralyzing force of fear. Fear breeds doubt and doubt cripples our ability to grow.

Many men are riddled with doubt. They doubt their ability, their intelligence, and their appeal. So often men are told as boys that they are not enough of this or too much of that. So as they grow they keep strengthening their inner narrative of "not enoughness." This plays a huge part in their relationship with failure. They are haunted by it. They will do whatever they can to avoid it and will over emphasize strategies and doing it "perfect" rather than simply going for it and learning along the way. It is good to have plans and strategies, but when they run a man and his fear of failure becomes crippling, he will often default to "paralysis by analysis" and in turn over analyze his life away, never really going for it, never really tapping into the full potential that can only come with taking the risks that are required in a life of purpose, self-growth and love. The result is a life that is one giant mental chess match that is lived solely in the mind and where his heart is rarely accessed.

If doubt cripples you, it owns you. Lost in an endless maze of "what if" scenarios your life will forever be on pause. What breaks down doubt and weakens its grip is committed action. Make a choice, with the best insights you can, and move forward. Take one step at a time. So often in life we want a giant spotlight to shine from where we are all the way to the end of our path. And yet, the best we often get is a dulled flashlight that can only shine on the next step. That's it. Stop waiting for a biblical insight that will bring you to your knees and illuminate your ultimate purpose in life. Does it happen to some? Yes. To most? Absolutely not.

For most, purpose and insight are not found, they are forged. They are forged with action that is doused with risk and the willingness to fail and learn. It is the only way. To doubt yourself is to doubt your brilliance and the magnificence bestowed to you by your creator. It is to sell yourself incredibly short and to settle for the crumbs of life when you deserve the entire loaf.

One of the greatest doubts that makes itself known in our thinking is the hesitation that has killed more dreams than falling short in results ever will. They are four simple words in our psyche, "What will people say?" These four words become an obsession of inevitability that we are leaving ourselves opened to being judged, criticized and joked about by our peers. This common narrative stops most men before they even start. In that moment, they become a prisoner. A prisoner to people's opinions, a slave to other people's fear and a robot to norms that were never designed to guarantee fulfillment.

The fear of being judged has crippled talented men for centuries. At the forefront of this fear is that if we evolved, grew and changed for the better that it would shift our relationships and possibly lose the affections of those closest to us. The fear is of being told "You're changing, I'm not sure I like the 'new you'." Men fear these words, and rather than take a risk to grow, they comply and opt for staying small so as to not disrupt the norm. Fearing the risk of losing love, they settle for mediocrity and status quo. *But this they forget; living the life that you truly desire does not alter your relationships, it reveals them.* If a man is generous with only $10 then he will be generous with $10,000,000. If a man is stingy with $10 he will also be stingy with $10,000,000. The amount simply highlights his already existing world. As you grow into your desired state, as you fulfill your destiny of being human, there will be those who cheer you on and champion you and there will be those who resist your growth and challenge you at every corner. The irony is, they are doing it already. Your success will simply highlight their jealousy or their encouragement. So why not go for your life with all that you've got? Instead of basing your future on the opinions of others, rise up to your own potential and let people have their opinions. It is time to close that chapter of doubt. The truth is that when a man really goes for what he wants, life will rise up to meet his commitment.

> *"And, when you want something, all the universe conspires in helping you to achieve it"*
> — Paulo Coelho

The fortitude that comes with clarity must first involve committed action. It is the willingness to try, to attempt, to adjust and to adapt with every effort. Otherwise, life will always be an empty hologram of what could have been.

Failure is a part of the journey. Your relationship with it will define how close you will come to your full potential. If you constantly doubt every move, every advancement, then typically under the surface of your actions is the fear that if you fail you will be less than, outcast, abandoned. This is simply not true. A man that is committed to his vision will summon a strength that can only be accessed by the whole-heartedly committed. Let discernment have a seat at your council but never let doubt have the final word. There are a million reasons why what you say you want is unattainable, laughable and unreasonable. But all it takes is one reason to actually go for it; to live a life of fulfillment without regret of what could have been, what you should have done and to actually live aligned to your deepest desires while being in service to your fellow man.

Demon #2 – Delay

> *"Every moment waited is a moment wasted, and each*
> *wasted moment degrades your clarity of purpose."*
> — David Deida

Great men do not second-guess themselves. They succeed or they learn. Either way, great men take action. Too often, we are clouded by confusion that results in hesitation and delay. This demon shows its head by getting us trapped in over-analysis and lost in vacuous amounts of data. When we hesitate, we lose energy that is irreplaceable. We miss the moment and the opportunities are lost. If timing is everything, then we failed at our attempt to strike swiftly and seal our fate with greatness.

The demon of delay hides behind a thick cloud of confusion. We tell ourselves we are not ready, that we need one more diploma, one more certification, and one more seminar and then we will "get it." And yet, over and over again we go forward not trusting ourselves and denying the idea that we could be an authority on our own life of purpose and fulfillment. We get trapped in the "not yet" game of convincing ourselves that there will be this biblical moment of clarity that will ensure us and validate us that we are ready and that we poses enough skill to dive in head first to our endeavors. Like the myth of one day, this "day of validation" is not coming either. We will never be fully ready because the journey forward is what shapes our growth and learning. If we hesitate, we stunt our growth and the concept of our fulfillment remains just that, a concept. We never have the experience of growth, success, failure, learning and adapting because we stay confused and locked in our fears of failure and what others might think. So, we continue building and adding to a tool kit whose blades stay sharp from being unused. Axes are meant to be swung and hammers are meant to strike. And while not every blow lands square at its mark, each swing is an attempt to build a foundation on which we can proudly rest our future.

We will never be 100% ready. Action is the antidote to delay. As we forge forward, with discernment, we commit to learning from our missteps and we celebrate our advancements, however big or small.

Demon #3 - Distraction

The demon of distraction is not hard to find in our culture today. We are constantly being marketed to of all the things that you "need" to feel complete. Rather than focus on your purpose in life, you are pitched distraction after distraction to trick you into short-term pleasures but long- term pains, constantly reminding you that you, as you are, are not enough. Just buy this product, this item, this thing, and you will finally feel wholeness and completeness. The strategy is brilliant and we fall for it constantly.

There is a high in distracting ourselves, let us not lie. The quick hit of dopamine we get from checking out, getting lost in other worlds that don't highlight our responsibilities feels good, but only for a short amount of time. Lack of discipline seems rewarding and liberating, but we must remember that the moments are fleeting. We must exercise vigilance that when we rest it is because we have earned the moment. Our purpose has been fed, our muscles exercised and hearts tired from giving our gifts. To rest is purposeful, but only after our purpose has been fueled. Why rest to store up energy that you do not plan on using except for repositioning the wasted energy of your distractions? Rest comes after action. Sleep comes after the movement and advancement of a purposeful day. To check out and give in to distractions with no meaningful work leaves the heart weary and the soul starving. We must adjust the equation to make rest purposeful rather than the easy way out or we will be so lost in confusion and laziness that we will think purpose and vision are privileges of the select few.

Being distracted feels good. But only for a moment. We get addicted to the checking of phones for likes and texts, listening to news viewpoints that we already agree with but don't challenge our own, checking out and numbing out so as to not face our day and responsibilities because our belief systems have convinced us that we can't handle all the possible situations that may confront us. And so we waste time. And energy. And we distract ourselves hoping it will all go away, the overwhelm of it all. We work hard during the week in pointless work only to escape on the weekends with alcohol and women. We enjoy the distracting "hit" for the moment but over time learn that we are left emptier than filled.

Distraction is a false high. It is the temporary hit of pleasure that never lasts. It feels good in the moment and then as it wears off, the chase begins again. We search for the next way to unplug and not feel the sense of overwhelm that comes with delaying our purpose. As we act on our distractions they become seductions and then we get lost in the fantasy of life rather than the tangible long-term gratification that comes with deliberate and committed action towards our goal. What we forget is that the energy it takes to check out and distract ourselves requires the same amount of energy to get back to center and refocus. If I am on a trail and venture 1 mile off the trail in a single direction then it is going to take me at least 1 mile of effort to simply get back to where I was. We forget that we are expending valuable energy that could have been far better used and in service to something greater in our lives.

In a time when news comes faster than it ever has, when opposing viewpoints revert to who can shout the loudest from their position, and where we are bombarded with the next latest thing to make your life better and save you time, it is easy to get lost in the overwhelm of keeping up. We lose sight of the simple moments of silence where we are alone with our thoughts and hearts and audit the slow and simple speed of nature and our life. It is rare today to be out of cell range and not have to compulsively check our phones for the latest update of drama and meaningless updates in the long run. To sit and contemplate seems to be a thing of the past, reserved for poets and philosophers. Let us not forget the value of unplugging and to work a purposeful day and let the company of family, friends and food be our only needed connection and entertainment.

There is a beauty in simplifying our lives from self-imposed or unconsciously welcomed distractions. As we clear out the superfluous of our lives we begin to remember the magic and meaning of this present moment now. It begins to fuel us from the spirit up and slows down our day to remember once again, that life is long. That we need not rush about our day to simply get to the next moment while missing the brilliant one in front of us. That life is more than keeping up with the latest trends and barrages of marketing but rather we have the power to be discerning of what we allow into our homes, our minds and our lives that is aligned with our purpose and inner desires. To be caught in distraction is to bury what it truly valuable in us and cloud our clarity of what ultimately makes us come alive.

NME Exercise:
Take an honest look at which demon(s) has or have a hold on you. Honesty is key if you truly want to shift and change your life. List the ways that you doubt yourself, delay your goals and distract yourself on a daily basis. Begin to make clear boundaries and agreements with yourself around these. Take small actions like setting deadlines and keeping them, making decisions and acting upon them and taking time away from things that you realize distract you. Small action over time will override and quiet the 3 D-emons.

Organize Your Inner World

We often give so much attention to our outer world, the space in which we inhabit, but so often disregard and ignore our inner world, the space that we live and create from. When our outer space is disorganized and chaotic we feel unsettled and not at ease, so we spring clean, we improve and we tidy up. This way, when someone asks where something is located, we know the direction to point him or her in effectively. Yet so often we overlook our inner world and leave it disorganized, unattended to and rarely give it the appropriate amount of attention. We forget that our inner world generates our reality and experience and not the other way around. If asked where courage is located internally, many men could only access it by chance or circumstance, forgetting that they have access to it in all moments. Without a relationship to that which is inside us, we get caught in the seeming randomness of our current states. We find ourselves wishing, hoping, even desiring to live and experience something new or in a new way.

When we give attention to our inner world and organize it, make it distinct, we begin to take the steps of mastering our state. We can then distinguish between personal power versus the need to force or control; clear becomes compassion rather than expectation; distinct is then long-term fulfillment rather than instant pleasure. We learn how to navigate our lives from the inside out instead of letting outside forces and outcomes define who we are, making a golden calf of our identities and accomplishments. Leadership is an inside game. Without access to your inner world you will be ineffective and your power will be diluted.

Tony Robbins tells one of my favorite stories. He insists it is from the founder of FedEx but others tie it to a printing company in Chicago. Regardless, the message is what is important. The story goes...

All of a sudden all the conveyor belts in the company plant stopped working. Shutting down all the progress and shipments going out. In a panic, the manager called a retired, long-time employee of the company and asked him to come help with the problem. Not far away, the ex-employee came to the warehouse and assessed the situation. Only after a few minutes he walked over to a box, turned a screw about a half turn to tighten it and in a second all the conveyor belts went back on and the work and order was restored. In just a few minutes, the man saved the company millions of dollars. Elated, the manager asked as he thanked him, "How much do I owe you?" To which the man replied "$10,000." The manager was puzzled and looked at the man and said, "You were only here for a few minutes and its $10,000? Perhaps you can get me an itemized bill and send me an invoice?" The retired worker looked at the manager and said that he could make him an itemized invoice right there on the spot. He grabbed a pen and a piece of paper and in less than a minute handed the invoice to the manager. The manager read it, smiled and went to the safe and handed the retired worker $10,000 cash. What did the bill say? What was so powerful on that note that convinced the manager in a moment that it was worth the cost? Simply this...

Turning screw = $1
Knowing which screw to turn = $9,999

For many of us, we've been "turning screws" our whole lives. It is rarely a lack of effort that doesn't have our lives go the way we want but rather a lack of understanding. To truly create the life that we desire we must understand the value of knowing which screw to turn. We must be able to look within ourselves and know what works and what doesn't; what the moment is calling for and when to access the inner states that will have us succeed in our missions.

One of your greatest powers as a human being is your ability to distinguish distinctions. To make something distinct is to highlight it and separate it from everything else; to have it stand out so that you can approach it from different angles, depths and perspectives. In doing so, you now have access to its power and usefulness. On the road, a green light is distinct from a red light. And knowing the difference between the two can save your life as a driver. If there were no distinction between red and green lights, driving would be a chaotic and dangerous endeavor.

Many of us in our culture have our inner world blended together. Where nothing is distinct and rarely anything internally stands out as important, valuable or even sacred. When our inner world is collapsed together, life will feel random at best and our results will be closer to luck than intentional. We must highlight, have stand out, that which we value, to create a life congruent with what we desire. This is the only way fulfillment will have footing; it must be built on an inner world that is uncompromising and fertile.

For instance, if I have compassion collapsed with expectation, I will limit my ability to love fully. In my inner world, to have compassion is to love someone where they are at in the journey of their life and consciousness. That requires patience, understanding, openness and willingness. If I have that blended together with expectation, meaning I will love them "as long as..." then I will be confused about the conditions that I believe they are not meeting in order for me to feel loved or give love. These are not the same thing. Expectations are conditions and concepts that I place on people and few ever even know about it. As long as they meet my expectations, I am happy and if they don't, I suffer. That gives the person all the power and takes it away from me and my ability to truly love. My conceptual expectations will override my actual experience of what is possible in that moment of relationship.

If compassion and expectations aren't distinguished in your inner world, you will be operating from an inner context that will continue to have disappointment show up in relationships. This is simply because they are not the same thing, although we operate as if they were. That would be as foolish and dangerous to say a red light and green light are the same to a driver.

To the degree that we have our inner world organized, we have the power to access what is needed and what the moment call forth from us. Being present gives us a doorway into our soul and the power that we can consciously create the lives, relationships and outcomes that we truly desire.

Distinction #1 - Masculine and Feminine

Masculine and feminine energy are equal but they not the same. Men and women are equal but they are not the same. Sameness and equal are distinct. Let's assert that all human beings have masculine and feminine energy. Neither is limited to sex, gender or sexual preference. Men and women are based on biology while masculine and feminine are based on energy. Men have both masculine and feminine energy as well as women have both masculine and feminine energy, just as the earth has a north and south pole that are opposites but work together. Typically, one energy is predominant until a person becomes what I call "fully integrated." But for now, let's assert that one energy tends to be a default. You can be a man and have dominant feminine energy and you can be a woman have dominant masculine energy. You can be a gay man and have dominant masculine energy and vice versa as well as a gay woman and have dominant feminine energy and vice versa. Again, it is not about sex or sexual preference but more about the prevailing energy that a person operates from. Both are equal, although not the same.

For now, let us distinguish masculine from feminine and use some concepts from David Deida's *Way of the Superior Man*.

Let's use the symbol for masculine energy as a mountain. The mountain is immovable; it stands strong, unwavering, and steadfast. Weather comes and goes and it does not bend or break. Its strength is commitment, striving, vision and we always know where we are in relationship to it. Masculine energy strengths are logic, reason, integrity, critical analysis and consistency. The ultimate goal for the masculine is freedom and purpose.

Let us now represent feminine energy as the ocean. It is expansive, deep beyond measure, a force of movement and power, it is ever changing (one day a lake, the next a tsunami), it is in constant movement and its depths can only be imagined. Feminine strengths are passion, inspiration, compassion, emotion, depth of feeling and connection. The ultimate goal for the feminine is intimacy and relationship.

Both energies are equal; both are needed to live a fulfilled life of connection and purpose. The masculine is about doing, the feminine is about being. Both are vital and necessary for fulfillment and power. If we are unaware of these distinct energies in our inner world, we will unconsciously default to one over the other even if the moment calls for the opposite.

When it comes to masculine and feminine energy we make several mistakes. First, we don't distinguish them. We don't explore the inner depths of ourselves and notice the polarities that we live within. Sometimes, needing to access logic and reason and other times needing to access passion and love. Without distinguishing them we tend to default to what we were taught growing up and let it become part of our personal and collective conditioning. We hear phrases such as "men don't cry," "don't let them see you sweat," "life is hard and you need to beat out the competition," etc. This lack of conversation has us default to what have been social norms based on gender rather than the inner energies of what works in the moment. If we default to logic (masculine energy) when the moment is calling forth compassion (feminine energy) then we will be ineffective and disconnected to the moment and our own inner power. We will end up trying to "fix" people when all they are asking for is a compassionate ear to listen with them. People won't feel heard, they won't feel listened to and connection will be lost and relationships will suffer. On the contrary, if life is calling forth masculine energy through commitment, integrity, determination and consistency to generate a project or a goal and you are accessing feminine energy through spontaneity and "going with the flow", then you'll wonder why your projects never get off the ground. We must be able to distinguish the polar energies within us so that we know what tools we have access to in any given moment. There will be times in life that call forth spontaneity, openness, "seeing where the moment takes you," and there will be times that call for you to be disciplined, steadfast, unwavering and committed. If you cannot distinguish for yourself what works and what is needed in that moment, then your potential will never be reached and your relationships will be strained.

The other big mistake we make with these polar energies is that we feel we must unconsciously choose one, masculine or feminine energy. To recognize that energies are distinct but then think we only have access to this or that, limits us. When this occurs we automatically default to the polar force that we are most familiar with from our conditioning. If we tend to be masculine dominant and take it to the extreme we will constantly default to logic, reason, strategy and we will inevitably default to trying to figure life out as though it were a mathematical equation. When we do this we cut off access to our emotion, to our heart and our inner fires and passion. We won't take risks in life because the proverbial numbers don't add up. We cut off trust and faith and even confidence because we will ultimately live from our heads and not our hearts. This extreme keeps us in our heads and life becomes an exhausting mental chess match of needing to know and calculate our every move.

If we tend to be more feminine dominant and constantly default to emotion, then we will be overly passionate and easily excitable but miss the vital components of consistency, dedication, strategy and detail. When we live in this extreme, we will start things in life and then stop as soon as it becomes hard, tiresome or boring. We will forfeit our commitments and instead do only what feels good to us in the moment. The problem with this is that when we choose to live a life of purpose and meaning, not everything is going to feel warm and cushy. Discomfort is required to live a truly fulfilling life. If we default too far to the feminine pole in our selves, then we will stop as soon as we are uncomfortable rather than push through with determination and perseverance to see our passions through. Life will be a constant ebb and flow of starting and stopping and self-sabotage will be littered throughout our lives. Projects won't come to completion and ideas and visions will remain dreams at best. And then we go to our graves never knowing our full potential.

Extremes are unsustainable. Too far left or right creates imbalance in the mind and body. If we unconsciously default to extreme masculine or extreme feminine within ourselves we will end up living only half full and true inner power will escape us. We will build homes with only half the tools rather than be aware that we have access to all the tools we need to create something extraordinary. Extremes have us cut off the opposite rather than use and utilize them effectively.

What is vital for our power is to first distinguish masculine and feminine energy. Once we make them distinct, rather than choose one or the other, the goal is to ultimately integrate them. To marry both into one human being is what creates balance, harmony and power. To be present enough to know what is the moment calling forth from you and then the willingness to access what is needed. If the moment is calling forth passion and inspiration then bring it, if it is calling forth steadfastness and logic then bring it. But you must be present to what is needed in each moment or else you will default to what is familiar. What is familiar is not what is effective. Doing what you have always done will get you what you've always had. It is now that we must, as men, become present to what works and what does not and incorporate the totality of who we are, both masculine and feminine energy. To deny one over the other is to live half full and half full and fulfilled are never going to add up.

As the masculine, your greatest power is your presence. The choice to be here and now; in this moment, connected. Most men in our culture today are going through the motions of what they think they ought to be doing or what they were taught to do and haven't questioned what they are actually doing in this moment now. As we mention all the ways we choose to be, our commitments and our goals of passion, purpose, freedom, fulfillment, power, trust etc., none of them are accessible without presence. Presence is the doorway in to being. Without it all our power remains conceptual and untapped. Presence invites us to be here and now, and from that place access and choose our inner states that are aligned to our visions, goals and desires. Without presence, keep dreaming. It is the opening to a life a freedom.

Presence is the power of the masculine and the feminine craves it. Let's go back to the analogy of the mountain and the ocean. The feminine, as the ocean, is continually fluctuating and unpredictable. It craves to know that the mountain is unmoving and unwavering in relationship to the oceans ebb and flow. The ocean desires to know its relationship with the mountain. Whether the ocean is high or low, it always knows and can trust that the mountain is unmoving. Presence is that power and element that the feminine craves. To access it and to be present through the feminine shifts, moods and changes is to practice a skill set that eludes the average man. To be present is to not need to fix and control everything, but to allow what is to unfold and then move forward based on commitment and honor of principles.

The New Man Emerging sees masculine and feminine energy as integral in his growth and evolution. Both are distinct, both equal and unique but not the same. To deny or suppress the feminine aspect of his soul and energy would be the ultimate disservice to the New Man Emerging. It would cut off his power and deny him his ultimate freedom. He sees and knows the ultimate benefit of marrying masculine and feminine, head and heart. He is present enough to dance between the two and knows when to bring out the hammer in his life or when to bring out the rose. His mastery is practiced through his presence and knowing how to access what is needed here and now and what the moment is calling forth from him. He does not run. He remains unmoving to life's challenges and rather than be a victim to his circumstances, he draws forth the tools that are eternally written in the DNA of his head and heart.

NME Exercise:

Determine what your dominant energy is. To achieve balance and power we must first see what your leading energy is and then balance it with the opposite. For the next few days notice you. Do you tend to lean towards getting results (masculine) or toward creating relationships (feminine)? Do you notice yourself defaulting to your mind and logic and figuring things out (masculine) or do you tend to feel things out and allow them to unfold (feminine)? There are plenty of quizzes and surveys online that you can test. Try a few and notice yourself and what your leading energy is. Then, seek to reach across from your strength and access the opposite energy so that you can move closer to integration and balance.

Distinction #2 - Principles

Our purpose shapes us and our principles guide us. An evolving man must be able to look within and know the principles that he lives his life by. As we aim toward a life of purpose we must have guideposts along the way. We must have inner boundaries that support us in achieving our goals; markers that ensure our safety and forward movement toward fulfillment. These inner guides and supporting benchmarks are our principles. Our principles protect our spirit and that which we value. And they are key to living a fulfilled and purposeful life.

If you have ever watched children go bowling, they often put up the bumpers in the gutters for them as the kids roll the ball forward. Why would we do this? We do it so that no matter where the child rolls the bowling ball, the bumpers ensure that he or she will at least hit something. Our principles are the inner "bumpers" of our lives. By being clear about them, we can ensure that as we move toward our goal of a fulfilled life, we are bound to hit something we are aiming at along the way. Without clear principles, a man won't be able to determine with clarity whether or not he is on track to hit his mark.

The New Man Emerging honors his principles. They are his lifeline to clarity and fulfillment. We must honor our principles and live and love them as though they are non-negotiable.

Our principles are the inner ways of being that we value most in life and experience. Principles, such as honor, integrity, authenticity, freedom, reverence, patience, etc. light the way for us. There are many states of being that are crucial to access from time to time, but your principles are the ones that stand out to you the most. They are the ones that you value above all else, the ones that you know in order to be happy and fulfilled, you simply couldn't live without accessing and exercising. They include appreciation, gratitude, consideration and respect. The list goes on, but you must determine what principles stand out to you the most. What would you stand for and even be willing to die for? If your principles were stripped from you it would be as though your soul was stolen away. We must realize that to live incongruent to our principles would be to go against the natural current of our life. For instance, if a man realizes that honesty is one of his guiding principles, he would then refuse to lie or tell mistruths. The value placed in honesty for him would dictate and determine his decisions and actions. If a man is unclear the value of his principle of honesty, he will sell out on himself and others, he will tell half-truths and manipulate himself to gain others approvals and affections rather than live and stand for what he believes is true and valuable in his hearts core.

As we evolve as men, we must first get clear on what we stand for and what principles we will use in operating in our lives. When we live within our principles and honor them, our lives move forward in a meaningful and purposeful direction. When we are unclear about our principles or we consciously live contrary to them, we suffer. Plain and simple. To live a life incongruent to our principles wreaks havoc in our relationships and results. It promotes chaos, uncertainty and stagnation. Our heart and soul suffer because we are denying who we truly are at our core and ignoring all the road signs that would lead us to peace and joy.

We do not change our lives and the world by our opinions. We change our lives and the world by our examples and committed actions. Therefore we must organize our inner world so that our principles are at the foreground of our hearts and who we are. They need to be accessible, within arm's reach of our spirit so that we can act in accordance to the core of our values. Inner disorganization and confusion will not produce the steadfast action that is required to advance the spirit and freedom of a man. Without access to your inner guides you will constantly be in a state of hesitation. Perhaps, even worse yet, you will be living contrary to your values and thus constantly cleaning up the collateral damage of your unconscious living.

The spirit of a nation, as well as man, begins to diminish the moment he adjusts his humanity to fit his politic rather than adjust his politic to fit his humanity. Too often we are moved by outside influences and we allow them to adjust our inner world and operate over our desired truths. We adjust internally rather than externally and we wonder why we are left lost, confused and unfulfilled. When we stand firm on the disciplined and principled footing of our inner world, our outer world begins to reflect it. We begin to shape our lives and our destinies from a higher order that is found within us. When we live free from the noise and chatter of external influences that do not seek to serve us, we begin to omit the distractions and seek to shape all the tasks at hand with the hands of guiding inner principles. We shape our lives by the hands inside us, not the other way around. When our inner world is organized and clear we become congruent to create the life results we truly desire. We become our own hero again.

For me, my principles are the guiding force in my life. They are non-negotiable. I refuse to compromise the inner elements that shape my life. This is not because I can't, but because I choose not to because I know the value that they bring to my life and the chaos that is caused by ignoring them. I have explored my principles in depth with various coaches and mentors; not realizing that my life seemed to constantly be cleaning up collateral damage due to a lack of organization of my inner world. Having discovered what is important to me internally, I have been able to cultivate the life and relationships that I have always desired.

To stay congruent and guarantee fulfillment in life we must first be clear about what our principles mean to us. Second, we must establish boundaries and rules so that we know when we are strengthening our principles or weakening them. These are our virtues. Virtues are behaviors that show high moral standards. I call these behaviors "therefores." "Therefore I do (or don't do)" certain behaviors or actions. We must first define what our principles mean to us and then establish our virtues. Behaviors that strengthen our spirit and moral center. Let me give you my personal principles and virtues...

****PRINCIPLES****

Humility – Humility to me is owning my accomplishments while praising and acknowledging the people and events that have assisted me in achieving them. It is to remind myself that I do nothing on my own without the support of others. Therefore, I refrain from bragging and boasting and I commit to going out of my way to thank people in their support.

Reverence – Reverence to me is to honor my place in nature and the circle of life. It is to remind myself that I am only on this earth temporarily and to bless the life force that I have been given. Therefore, I spend at least one hour per day outside in nature undistracted.

Simplicity – Simplicity to me is not taking anything more than I need. It is to refrain from gluttony. Therefore, I do not overeat, buy anything without function or meaning and keep my living space uncluttered.

Patience – Patience to me is being content in this moment here and now. Therefore I do not panic or rush to frustration.

Honor – Honor to me is living in accordance with my principles and respecting my relationships. Therefore, I refrain from knocking people down. I refrain from gossip, and I abstain from pornography and any violence especially as it pertains to women.

<u>Gratitude</u> – Gratitude for me is to be appreciative for each moment and seek to create value in all circumstances no matter what. Therefore, I refrain from complaining.

<u>Compassion</u> – Compassion to me is loving people exactly where they are at in their journey. Therefore, I do not try and change people and refrain from judging people's beliefs or ways of living.

<u>Forgiveness</u> – Forgiveness to me is to live with grace from a clear space that is new in this very moment. Therefore, I do not hold grudges and lock people or myself in the past.

These are the principles by which I live my life. I am not perfect or 100% in them each day. Though I hold them as the gold standard in which I live my life. Sometimes my principles are challenged, other times they are polished. However, they are always at the foreground of my life and consciousness. I have learned, through experience, that when I live by them I feel a deep sense of freedom, self-esteem and fulfillment. And when I don't, my life suffers tremendously and I am no longer the hero in my own life. At the foreground, they become the benchmark to which I filter all my actions and behaviors knowing that they are my greatest ally on my journey to awakening.

Without inner principles, we get lost, and life begins to unravel randomly and chaotically. Principles are the guides that we need to get clear and to ensure that we advance in the evolution of our character. To be the hero in your own story it must be your character that grows, not just your accomplishments. Accomplishments without character leads to shallowness and lack of fulfillment. Character with accomplishment leads to leadership and contentment in one's self and journey. You have no greater compass available to you and your inner world than that of setting forth true and clear principles of that which you value and live your life by.

NME Exercise:

Get clear on your inner principles. List or find a list of principles online. Try to get at least 25 principles. Then narrow them down to the top 8-10 that you find most valuable; the ones you feel you could not live without. Then take those 8-10 principles and define them for yourself. They may match the dictionary version or they may be completely unique to you. Either is fine. Then, after you define them write next to them your "therefores." What are the behaviors you do or do not do to strengthen that principle? Keep your list visible to you so that you can see it each day to remind you of what is important to you in creating your life.

"This and other exercises and concepts in this section were introduced and/or clarified to me by Gary Grant of Heroic Life Strategies."

Distinction #3 - Commodities

A commodity is something useful or valued. We tend to look at commodities externally; that which we own, possess or acquire. However, we have inner world commodities that are beyond a price tag that we often give little to no attention. If we are to shift our perspective from that which we externally "own" to that which we inwardly "possess", then our lives take on an entirely new shape and meaning. Imagine if we were to operate our inner world and balance our inner state as effectively as our checkbooks. We would take more care and attention knowing that inner foundations are what we build the quality of our lives on. Shifting our perception from "we are the culmination of our external achievements, accumulations and statuses" to the perception that "we are the make-up of our inner states, principles and inner expressions" allows us to live a life that comes from creativity and desire, rather than a scarce platform of external situations and identities. For this to take place, we must highlight and examine and bring to the foreground that which we use and value, our inner commodities, and allow them to be the driving force in our lives.

*Our three greatest inner commodities are
our time, our love and our energy.*

Time is one of the most valuable assets that we have. Time is also one of the most wasted things that we unconsciously give away. If you ever question how great a commodity time is, ask any man on his deathbed. He will set you straight on time's value. No one has ever come to the end of his life and regretted not spending more time in the office or slaving over his "to-do lists." Rather a man regrets the time he wasted not being present with his family and the times he refused to feed his creative ideas that he was too afraid to bring to life. And he certainly wonders about the risks that he failed to take, rather than the things he attempted and fell short of.

We give away this precious commodity of time in our laziness, our delay and procrastination with the idea that there will somehow be a better day, a better time when all our conditions and circumstances will line up and be ideally in our favor. We fall for the myth of "one day." The truth is, one day you will be dead. And it will be up to you to calculate the time you wasted or the time you lived well spent. Falling for the myth of more time has us miss the magic, possibility and aliveness of this very moment.

There is no greater time than now because there IS no time but now. This may initially sound cliché, but here is a simple test: raise your hand when the future comes. You will sit with your arms at your side for the rest of your life. The future is not coming; the future is determined in this moment, the one that you sit in right now. The choices and actions you make and take in this moment are the words you are writing to the next chapters of your life. Your future is determined right now. Will it be a future of action, principle, value, creativity and fulfillment? Or will it be laced with procrastination, waiting, hoping and over-analyzing? One actionable step toward your vision is worth more than all the data of the attempted plotting of your future. Your analysis and calculations are erased the day you take your last breath while your committed actions echo into eternity. Your choice.

The concept of "time management" is actually a falsehood. You cannot manage time. Time is time. How you manage yourself **IN** time is going to make all the difference in the world. Dedicating your time to what makes you come alive, spending time with people you love, learning and growing from the things that you always wanted to know and experience will make you happy, whole and fulfilled. It is easy to become overwhelmed by the projection of the future. It looks vast, uncertain, and chaotic. That is why how you manage yourself today becomes the culmination of tomorrow's state and destiny. Remember, It is easy to look at the ocean and be blown away by its size and grandeur. But when broken down, the ocean is drops of water and life is moment-to-moment choices.

When we manage our choices in the present moment and filter them through our principles and stay present to the magic of this moment now, we shape our future and destiny congruent to our internal state. We take charge of creations in life and live from a place undeterred by outside events and circumstances and live a life that is deliberate and purposeful. How will you choose to live? What is the future that you desire to be manifest inside and outside of you? All that you answer is determined in the commodity of time and that which you choose here and now!

Love is un-definable. It is the force that permeates and penetrates the evolution and advancement of the human soul. Though ungraspable in words, it is a commodity that we possess even though it eludes our words. Love is like the wind, even though we can't see it, we can always witness its effects. We can clearly see in our lives the outcomes of where love is given or withheld. To love is to fuel every motion with magic and transform the mundane into something special and sacred. To withhold love is to cut off the oxygen to the fire that will give your existence purpose and life.

When we withhold love, we diminish our ability to forgive, to show compassion and ultimately to grow as a human being. We justify withholding love due to past hurts, pains and experiences. Although we forget that in our justification we are damaging our own spirits and stunting the growth of our power to lead, learn and love deeply. We devalue our greatest commodity by setting up illusionary boundaries and concepts of love that we have confused with the experience of love. We make check lists and score cards in relationships that ultimately state "I will love you as long as ..." "My needs are met, you love me the way I want, you do this and don't do that." This is not love but rather conditions of love. Which turn relationships from "I love you very much" to "I trade you very much." I trade you that I won't touch this wound in you if you do not touch this one in me. Relationships become more of a negotiation than a place of true healing and growth. Love is beyond conditions and grows and deepens in the space of the unknown and the connection to the present moment.

To love conditionally is to limit your capacity to truly give and receive. Loving "as long as" will only strengthen your existing paradigm but not support growth outside your limiting concepts. To love deeply, unconditionally, unequivocally is to tap into the very soul of the human experience and allow its force to shape you into the mold of life's choosing. It is to risk, to suffer, to expose yourself to the world and let the pain of expansion do its will. It will break the chains and fragments of your false identity and leave you questioning every limit you ever placed on yourself, your woman and the world. The gift is to revel in the stretching of the unlimited expansion and potential of love. To know its depths are unreachable and yet still chase it with passion is to bring life into every breath that you take. To withhold it and to question your ability and capacity to love will atrophy your spirit and leave you stuck inside your box and comfort zone and give you nothing but an illusion of love's possibility.

Give it now, in this moment, in all that you do and love with an abandon that will be insurmountable. Start with those around you and spread it like the wind spreads seeds of wildflowers. The wind doesn't decide what seeds go where but rather gives of its power and lets the seeds fall where they may. The joy of the wind is not in where it brings the seeds, but rather in the dance the seeds partake in.

❦ ❦ ❦

Energy can neither be created nor destroyed. But it can be wasted. Too often, men today are putting their energy and efforts into the very things that deplete them, burn them out and chip away at their very spirits. They spend their days slaving for another's dream rather than their own. They spend their lives lost in their tasks without the ability to see from a higher perspective where they are headed and aimed. They give up their health and relationships that are designed to nurture them while being in the pursuit of status and external validations. Days turn into decades and they are left confused about where their life went.

Where our focus goes, our energy flows. A man lit up by his passion and purpose will tap into a realm of energy that seems limitless. Whereas the man who has compromised his spirit and dreams will operate with an invisible weight that plagues him and keeps his energy sluggish and his power diluted. Your dreams require your energy. You vision demands of you your focus and commitment to move outside your comfort zone and risk your limits for something far greater. You were not designed to be born a slave but rather a unique contribution to the world around you. Small and subtle compromise of energy and spirit day after day is a plague of the modern man. Promises of security and status only seem greater temporarily than the energy of freedom and self-reliance.

We give away our day to tasks and to-do-lists not realizing we defer our dreams along with them. It is time to reclaim our energy and become the protectors of our focus. To master this moment so that it is aligned with our destiny of tomorrow requires attention and intention. That nagging in you of something greater will never go away, you mine as well feed it. Like a pilot light that won't snuff out or extinguish, it is up to us to fuel your inner fire with your mental, physical, emotional and spiritual energy. Life, all in, is easier lived than life at 90%.

Audit your day. Audit your every move and ask yourself "Is this essential to the life I truly desire?" If so, continue to give it all the energy required. If not, begin to strip it away from your daily life. Knowledge is in acquiring, wisdom is in shedding what is non-essential. Only you can close your own eyes at night and answer the question of whether your energy was best utilized in this day. Was your day spent on purpose or was your energy distracted by shiny objects and tasks that make no dent in eternity? Did you give freely of all your commodities or did you withhold them, storing them up for some imaginary future? Did you live deliberately and remind the people in your life of their value and their contribution in your life of purpose?

So many people are paralyzed in jobs, relationships and positions where they don't belong. Run every scenario you are in through your commodities like a filter.

Is what I am doing (or who I am with) worth my valuable time?
Is what I am doing (or who I am with) an expression of my love?
Is what I am doing (or who I am with) giving me energy?

We must ask these questions of ourselves and we must be willing to walk away from anything that is not a "yes" to all 3. 2 out of 3 won't do. We must be willing to put our heart and soul into all that we do so that when we die, we die on empty with all our gifts given. Do not confuse this with "everything should be easy." It shouldn't be and it won't be. Even in our most challenging moments of living a life of purpose, we must still be able to answer all 3 questions with confidence.

The nagging won't go away. This is not a threat but a warning that your spirit demands of you your very best. If you were to die today would you be satisfied? Would you die on empty with all your gifts given and dreams fulfilled? With honest reflection, inquire about where it is that you spend your valuable energy. Like a sacred account, be diligent where you spend this currency. It is possible to close your eyes at night and be unable to sleep with the excitement of a child on Christmas Eve because of the positive anticipation of tomorrow. It is another opportunity to give, to receive and to live with a sense of magic and fulfillment and to anticipate the day to come with an alignment of you're very soul in your life's work. Your freedom and aliveness depend upon the deliberate focus of your energy here and now.

NME Exercise:

In a notebook make 3 columns signifying your 3 commodities. Make them distinct; TIME, LOVE, ENERGY. Honestly list in all 3 categories what is <u>getting</u> your attention and what you <u>wish</u> was getting your attention. Ask the 3 questions of all that is getting your attention.

> *Is what I am doing (or who I am with) worth my valuable time?*
> *Is what I am doing (or who I am with) an expression of my love?*
> *Is what I am doing (or who I am with) giving me energy?*

Take a look at your lists and notice what changes you need to make. Don't wait, make the adjustments immediately.

Distinction #4 - Vigilance to Commitment

Average people run their lives based on their circumstances. Extraordinary people run their lives based on their commitments. The New Man Emerging is a man that honors his commitments. Circumstances and conditions fall short as excuses for why he can't achieve what he desires. When we organize our inner world we find that commitment becomes the greatest fuel for generating and creating the life we truly desire.

Commitment is all in. There is no back door. We give it all we have and either win or learn. When we give our word to something or someone and we make it happen, we develop personal power and self-esteem. We build up equity of inner confidence that has us trust and believe that we are capable of creating the life of vision that we say we want. What separates the great men from average is vigilance to commitment. It eliminates the default to excuses as to why we cannot have or achieve what our heart is called to. Instead, commitment encourages us to re-shape and redesign the very being in who we are to have what we desire happen.

Too often we attend the seminar, the class, the weekend retreat and we are fired up and riding high only to allow the feeling to wear off as time goes by. Then we seek the next course, the accreditation, and the next certificate to validate the time we have put in, only to get caught in the constant seeking of the "next thing." Then after we complete it, we let our foot off the gas and get caught in the trap of compiling experiences without actually integrating them into our daily lives.

The New Man Emerging does not give himself the luxury of complacency. The weekends and workshops are great but they only last to the level in which we are committed to adjusting and reshaping our everyday habits and rituals. There is no sense in putting new insights and practices on top of an old operating system that is broken. Commitment to growth is the very element and characteristic that distinguishes exceptional from average. And the New Man Emerging is exceptional. He leads his life, not by the chasing of the high, but by the polishing of the ordinary and mundane, thus making it effective, powerful and useful to himself and all others.

Discipline and commitment generate freedom. This seems like a contradiction but stay with it for a moment. The man that is disciplined develops a skill that promotes mastery. Which is the opposite of our current culture of immediacy and instant satisfaction. Take for instance a boy that is bullied as a kid. He then decides to learn a martial art and dedicates a decade of his life to becoming a black belt. 10 years later, that same boy, now perhaps a man, is free. He knows how to meet any circumstance, even dangerous ones, with skill and discernment. It was his commitment to learn, to practice and a willingness to fail along the way, that generated his inner freedom that he now experiences. Without a commitment, he would have stopped, he would have given in to the excuse that it is too hard, too long or that something else was more important than his own desire for inner freedom.

We think, or are taught, that freedom is doing what we want, with whom we want, whenever we want. But consider for a moment, that if we operated our lives this way, we would actually feel depleted and unfulfilled. If you were to eat whatever you want, sleep whenever you want, work and drink whatever you want for one week, you would actually be left exhausted. On the contrary, if you ate nutritious foods, disciplined your water intake, worked an appropriate number of hours, rested each night and prioritized your sleep as well as make time in your life and week for relationships and leisure you would be left feeling energized and fulfilled. Vigilance to commitment generates freedom rather than chasing fleeting pleasures from moment to moment that wear off due to lack of earning our endeavors.

Commitment must be distinguished and at the foreground of our hearts. Otherwise we will become lost in circumstances of delay and fall victim to the conditions of our life. Commitment stretches us to redesign the very core of who we are. It allows us to grow past our self-imposed limits and invites us into greater possibilities of life and experience. Without vigilance to our inner commitments we will become trapped in mediocrity while wondering why our lives are un-enriched. We must presence our commitments and remain vigilant to them so as to rise above the doldrums of average and mediocre.

NME Exercise:

For one week, notice any place that you fall short in your commitments. Do so from a place of non-judgment and notice for yourself what got in your way of having what you say you want to happen. Was it a sense of security that had you not take a risk? Perhaps, it was too uncomfortable to adjust yourself to make it happen. Or perhaps you gave in to your belief system that told you that you couldn't do it. Just notice for yourself what got in the way that had you break any commitments and then examine for yourself where else that same theme shows up for you in your life and journey and what you are missing out on because of it.

PURPOSE VS. PLATFORM

In our search for success, we have lost the pursuit of purpose and fulfillment. For the New Man Emerging, his purpose is his ultimate goal. Fueled by freedom and directed toward the vision he has for his life and the world he aims all that he has; his gifts, talents, skills and focuses all of them in the direction of what breathes life into that "unique fire that burns in his heart." Anything short of living a life "all in" won't suffice. He is a man that is determined to create results while cherishing the relationships he builds along the way to the mountain summits of his dreams.

Far too often in today's world, men are sold the idea that their purpose in life is to work, provide and advance in some imaginary ladder of success; thus confusing their purpose in life with work or their job. Over time, work becomes their identity, the very thing that they allow themselves to be defined by. It is not uncommon for today's man to ask another his name shortly followed by "What do you do?"; as though the answer to that question would answer who that man is. It answers what he does, not who he is at the core of his soul. It doesn't answer what lights him up, what he wakes up for and what will be written on his tombstone because of how he lived and what he contributed. As this work identity builds and gets stronger, todays man's spirit begins to fade and the risks he is willing to take become too great and too out of reach, enabling him to opt for comfort and conformity rather full self-expression and freedom.

The New Man Emerging is led by purpose, not by comfort. In fact, he recognizes and welcomes the fact that discomfort is the price of admission for living a fulfilled and purposeful life. To the degree that we default to comfort, we become deaf to the whisper of wildness and adventure in our hearts, spending our days fulfilling someone else's dream and trading true freedom for a 401k.

One of the remedies of this predicament is to distinguish **Purpose** from **Platform**. Far too many men are living as though what they "do" is who they "are." The challenge with this is over time what you do becomes your identity. Then getting a job, better yet a career, becomes some kind of guarantee of happiness and fulfillment. But too often these daily workings have us diminish the fire inside. It is as though you were put here on earth to only meet deadlines. What you do is NOT your purpose in life, it is your platform in life, and those two things are not the same.

Your purpose in life is the very thing that you would have define your life. The one state, cause or way of being that you desire to leave the world with after you are gone. "Here lies (insert your name), he was a man of (insert your purpose). When you look back on your life, what would you want to be known for? What contribution would you make because you lived? Imagine money and time and family were no limitation; that you were free to live from your heart's core. What would that etching on your tombstone say? Represent? Acknowledge?

For me, it is "healing". That is my main function and goal in this life. To be a healer of mind, body and spirit. All the ways that I do that are my platforms; author, coach, speaker, spouse, friend, brother and son. It is not my purpose in life to be an author but rather that is my platform. Author is a vehicle in which I deliver my purpose of healing.

Too often men collapse their platform as their purpose in life, thus leaving them unfulfilled and questioning, "Is this all I was put on earth to do?" It is as though your life were to be slaved five days of the week with a douse of freedom on the weekend as you balance excitement with catching up on sleep from the previous days. And eventually over time, you run a sufficient deficit of energy and passion. Even the platform you currently have or seek is not your purpose, it is your vehicle. Whether you are attorney or you cut lawns doesn't matter, neither one is your purpose in life, it is your platform. The question is, is the platform you are choosing congruent and aligned to your purpose? Or do you find yourself on a daily basis bending your inner ethics and principles to make money and maintain your way of living? Answer these questions honestly for yourself so that you can begin to discover and shape the life that you are truly designed and destined to live. A man without a purpose becomes lost and will live his life searching for fulfillment in destructive behaviors, if he isn't in connection to his soul's true desire.

The New Man Emerging is a contribution. His life is dedicated to giving his gifts to the world in a creative way or a humble way that serves far more than his comfort and security. When the United States' was attempting to put a man on the moon in the 1960's, everyone that worked at the NASA department all answered the "What do you do here?" question the same exact way. They all answered, "I'm putting a man on the moon." Whether they worked in the control room or mopped the floors, all the employees were part of a greater vision, and all played a role. The work was secondary to the vision. The platform served a life of possibility, creativity and exploration. When a man loses sight of his purpose and vision he will be left to living a life of mediocrity that tends to default to people pleasing and deferred dreams. It is the sure fire path to resentments.

If you have not discovered, or possibly had the courage to admit to yourself what your purpose in life is, that is ok, but you must begin now. You must not delay in this. A man without purpose is like a fire without oxygen. Fulfillment in life will have no place to grow without a purpose to aim it at. Explore the world within yourself and be true to what you find. What will be written on your tombstone because you had the courage to go after it and make it the driving force in your life? What will be the very thing worthy of you giving your life over to? What gift will death seek when he comes to your door only to find it completely given? The question is not if and when is death coming, the question is what will be the message and contribution of your life the moment death inevitably comes to your door?

NME Exercise:

To get clear on your Purpose make it as simple as possible. Sit for a few minutes with your eyes closed and take a few deep breaths. Now imagine you are standing over your own gravestone. What does it say? "Here lies (your name) he was a man of _____." What is the blank that you fill in?

For instance, "Here lies Michael, he was a man of healing." Healing is my ultimate aim. It is what I direct all the actions of my life toward.

What do you want your life to be about? What is the experience that you want your life to fulfill? Look at what you do day-to-day and begin to strip away and eliminate anything that doesn't align to that purpose.

PART 2

CHASING GRIZZLIES

I believe there is a calling in the hearts of all men to leave the noise, the traffic and the distraction of society behind and stand in nature on his own two feet and experience the depth of strength that God has given him.

As I stood at the water's edge overlooking the landscape of giant mountains, sky and colors I was speechless. I had an easier time believing that what I was witnessing in front of me was a scene more painted by spirits than some scientific explanation of plate movement under the earth's crust. I was moved by the way the rows and layers of mountains and water came to a single point as though they agreed on meeting at this one sacred location. This was a place that was hauntingly beautiful and the reason I stood there with my two brothers was even more haunting. It was to honor our dad's final wish to have his ashes scattered among the mountains and tall trees. Only months before, as his health was ailing him, he made me promise him that I would put his remains in a special place where his spirit could roam free and he could watch the changing of the seasons while the mountains dwarfed all the other life forms around. What better place could that be than Montana?

My dad was a big outdoorsman. His ideal vacation would be horseback riding in the Rocky Mountains, boiling river water, sleeping on the ground next to his old Weatherby rifle after a long day of being sun kissed and shaded by the mountains. Growing up with stories of adventures in the wild fueled me as a young boy and there is no doubt that my love of nature, and time spent in the woods, was seeded in me by dad. He hunted any chance he could as I was growing up on the east coast, but it was the trips to the Rockies that excited him the most. He hunted elk, deer, sheep, antelope and anything that could draw him west to the great mountains. And he got them all, except one, the grizzly bear.

The grizzly always eluded my dad. However many times he tried, it would always escape him. Too far for a shot or just too hidden to capture, he never got the animal he was always so spiritually drawn to.

I remember being in the hospital while he was still conscious. He made me promise him that I would take his remains to Rockies and scatter his ashes there. Even in his state, he said it with so much conviction as though he knew there was a greater purpose to his request. Not long after that moment, he lost consciousness and I would never speak to him again.

After a day on oxygen and the tension of waiting mixed with inevitability and uncertainty, my step mother whispered in my father's ear and assured him we would all be ok, that it was ok for him to go on. As though scripted on queue, a nurse came in from outside the room that was monitoring his vitals and informed us he was passing on. Rather than cry, rather than resist, I grabbed my father's hand and began shouting at him with a simple command, "do not turn around, keep going, go get him, your grizzly is waiting for you!"

TRUST YOUR MEDICINE

"You must learn to get in touch with the innermost essence of your being. This true essence is beyond the ego. It is fearless; it is free; it is immune to criticism; it does not fear any challenge. It is beneath no one, superior to no one, and full of magic, mystery and enchantment."
— Deepak Chopra

Contrary to most schools of thought, your purpose in life is not found; it is forged, cultivated and generated. Remember "Question 1?" ("How well did you tend to that unique fire that I put inside your heart?") That fire is your purpose. It is the uniqueness of you that only you possess. "Finding" your purpose is built upon the assumption that you don't already have it written on your soul's DNA. It suggests you must go somewhere outside of you to find or be deemed worthy of receiving your purpose. It creates pressure and a state of anxiety for many men because they are always looming with the question "What if I don't find it? What if I fail or fall short?" To forge your purpose or to cultivate it suggests that you already possess it. That it is already within you and that it must not be found but rather fed. Like a pilot light that has laid dormant but not extinguished, it simply requires a fueling so that it can grow.

So many men have walked into my office carrying a weight on their hearts with the same line, "I need to find my purpose" or sadly admitting "I feel like I have no purpose in life." It is not uncommon today. So many of us have compromised our spirits for safety and security, not realizing that the fire in us will never be fed by our conformity. For the New Man Emerging, to live without purpose is like a fire trying to burn without oxygen. It simply won't work. Purpose fuels his every action including whom he chooses to be in relationship with. Without this clarity, men feel lost, searching and medicating with temporary fixes without ever getting to the core of what is truly in their heart and how they truly desire to live their lives. Without purpose, life will always feel empty.

Many men won't even admit they already know their purpose in life. Afraid of being judged or not being worthy of their own inner fire keeps men from truly living from a deep, meaningful place within themselves. Other men fall into the category of being confused about their purpose and end up building a mental paradigm that keeps them trapped in an endless searching for it. This is where I work with individuals on a process I call "Trusting Your Medicine."

Your medicine is the culmination of your intuition mixed with your unique gifts. It is the impulse that arises within you and reveals itself as the desire to create. Your medicine is your spiritual fingerprint. In the east, it is called your Dharma. Let's come from the perspective that that unique fire is already in you and that it was placed in you by your higher source, the moment you were born or even before. You have a sacred contract with all of life and have a unique gift that only you possess. And like the DNA of humans that is predominantly the same, there is a small difference, a minute fraction that makes you unique from everyone else. From this perspective, there is nothing to seek or find. There is simply a choice to express it. It simply becomes the question of whether you will feed it or fight it. Will you fuel it or let it go unfed?

This idea is a departure from our norm. In a time when so much focus is external, where we are being marketed to constantly about things outside of us that promise to bring us happiness; the next latest thing, the picket fence and the ideal love. It seems to never stop. But what we are pointing at here is that none of that matters without first tapping into the medicine already in you. The fire in you and the uniqueness that you possess is not to be feared, denied or hidden, but rather it is to be expressed and celebrated.

In a tribe, all have roles and functions that celebrate the individual while strengthening the whole. To "fit in" is to confidently recognize your function through your gifts and talents, not to lose spirit and compromise who you are for approval. This is vital to see because to live with a compromised spirit is to live less than your potential, rather than allow your medicine to evolve and be expressed creatively. Without your medicine being fueled, it will grow frustrated and express itself destructively. Like a volcano under pressure your medicine is going to come out one way or the other: either creatively or detrimentally. Using your gifts to build something of value in the world is a huge component of the masculine heart. To suppress it will often lead to compulsion and addiction that is rooted in unexpressed potential energy. It will come out as anger, depression, frustration, perfectionism and addiction. These all become masks to a spirit that has lost its way from joy and full self-expression and clings to false identities that only temporarily soothe but cause collateral damage and harm in the long run.

To trust your medicine is to surrender to a process of awakening to the fire already in you. To recognize and connect with something greater than your everyday concerns and live from a place that is truly fulfilling and meaningful. To do otherwise, is to sell yourself and the world short of your potential.

Phase 1 - Connect with It

The first step to Trusting Your Medicine is to connect with it. It is the unique fire that is in you, that burns at the root of your soul. As men we are taught that this is a thing, a status, an accomplishment. But deeper than that, these accomplishments are actually symbolic of experiences or inner states. When I ask men "What would you do if money and time were not a factor?" Often they will give an example of a platform that they feel would be ideal for them. For example, they will tell me that they would love to be a public speaker to youth or to design something that supports the community, be an entrepreneur, or do charity work for the less fortunate. My follow up question is then, "What is the experience that you associate with that?" This is when they say "freedom," "inspiring others," "unity and bringing people together." This is where, sometimes unbeknownst to them, they actually begin getting clearer on their purpose.

Purpose is a state, an experience that the soul yearns to generate and create for others as well as experience for itself. From the purpose of "inspiration" a man can develop countless platforms in which to deliver it. If we narrow down a man's purpose to "inspiring others" than we can begin to examine the platforms best suited for him to do so. Examples include writing, speaking from stage, creating a group etc. He can aim all his intentions, actions, choices, even relationships at this one goal and he can connect to the medicine that is already in him. After that, it becomes possible and clearer to develop a lifestyle around this one aim. Without it, his actions will be diluted and never hold the true power as a man on a mission with a clear goal and intention.

What keeps us from connecting to our purpose? It is easiest to say "confusion." But typically deeper than that just below the surface is the poison of fear. When we look deeper than the confusion of "I just don't know what my purpose is" it becomes revealing and evident that there is fear clouding and muddying the waters of insight. One of the biggest reasons, when we are truly honest, is the fear of "what will people think?" This question that we obsessively ask ourselves has killed more dreams than failure ever will. We become paralyzed by it and the hypothetical outcomes of its answer keeps us trapped, stagnant and confused.

When we shift our focus from the opinions and judgments of others, we can begin to get clear on what it is that makes us come alive. We are unique to ourselves, not needing the approval and permission of society and others to tell us what we should do or how life is supposed to be lived. We can connect with our hearts desires and truly live from a place of fulfillment and meaning that is beyond our presuppositions of how it should look. It requires us to take a risk, to possibly fail and to grow from what we learn along the way. This is truly the journey that shapes us. But it must start from a place that is clear and connected to something greater than our fear, our need of approval and our fear of failure. A man loses his way the moment he loses his "why." Without a clear "why" that he is connected to, his actions become fruitless and lacking the proper amount of depth and substance.

All men, including great men, have fear. Waiting for it to dissolve or go away is a pointless and hopeless endeavor. Growth and advancement come from connecting with something greater than our limitations and making a committed advancement towards it, even if it is just a single inch. Connect with the fire inside you. Trust your medicine and all the unique gifts that you have been given to make your purpose present. Fuel it, feed it and follow it to wherever it leads you.

Phase 2 - Own It

One of our greatest misfortunes as human beings is our denial of our own true self. The gift of divinity and greatness within us is not to be ignored, denied or delayed. We spend so much of our lives ignoring the true inner nature of our own power and wisdom; not trusting ourselves and our connection to nature and God. By doing so, this leaves us cut off, disconnected, living under our potential and diluted. For the New Man Emerging, his medicine is not a curse, it is a gift to be opened and owned.

The interesting thing about gifts is that they are only valuable when you open them and when they are given. If you don't own your medicine that would be the equivalent of wrapping presents for your children on their birthday and then not letting your kids unwrap them. It sounds cruel when we put it that way, but that is exactly what we do when we withhold from others, especially the people we love.

Somewhere along the way our culture collapsed being "humble" to playing "small." The common inner belief of talented men is that they don't want to outshine anyone else. They think by doing so it would mean upsetting other people, stealing the spotlight, making other people uncomfortable and have themselves look arrogant.

The irony is that by withholding our gifts, withholding our medicine, we are the ones that are actually being selfish and arrogant, because people don't get to mutually benefit by the unique fire that is in us. People miss out on our power, wisdom, clarity, insight, creativity and all the states that they yearn for from us. But we withhold from people because we are too concerned with the opinions of others. They may call us cocky, arrogant, a "know-it-all" and many of us, up until this point, haven't been brave enough to take that risk.

But who are you not to be an authority in your life? Your gifts are unique to you, your soul, your spirit, your fire. Only you can connect with the divine cord within you and live from a place where that is fed and expressed through your life. It is not for others to give you, it is for you to own. Only you can unlock your own authenticity. You are the hero in your story and it must come from a place of ownership to truly unlock its full potential and power.

Does this mean bragging and boasting? Most certainly not. The New Man Emerging is a man of confidence mixed with humility, a man of clarity and directness that delivers his words with potency as well as sensitivity; like an arrow to another's heart with the intention for the center to bloom into a new possibility. True greatness steals nothing from another person. It builds others up and allows everyone's fire within to burn brighter than the previous flame. The need and compulsion to brag comes from a wound of insecurity to aggrandize ones self and give a brief sense of superiority and significance. Arrogance is the camouflage of insecurity. For the evolving man this is simply unfulfilling and pointless. Fleeting moments of significance are useless compared to his true sense of purpose that require his inner most strengths and gifts. His medicine speaks for itself.

When we own our medicine and commit to cultivating and feeding it, we tap into a new framework for living and giving. We begin to give up the search for happiness and the need for external approval and shift our focus onto what is already present within us and yearns to come forward and be expressed. Rather than demand that life bring us certain inner states, we can instead choose the states that are already present and we can bring them to life. We can become the true author and generator of our state and story and begin to craft a life that is in alignment with our true worth and authenticity. Will people still have opinions? Certainly. Will they matter? Most definitely not. When a man is focused on his goal and aim and harnessing his inner tools to reach his potential, he does not waste energy on anything that seeks to distract him. Lions do not concern themselves with the opinions of sheep. Ownership lays the groundwork and sets the framework for full potential and the New Man Emerging knows that the world or his heart, will not accept anything less.

Phase 3 - Give it

The spiritual law of giving and receiving is incredibly important as well as misunderstood. To give is to reinforce having. To withhold our gifts causes stagnation and hesitation in life. In order to ensure and experience our medicine we must in fact give it.

In the physical realm, if I give you $100 you now have $100 more and I have $100 less. That is a physical law. As one side increases the other side decreases. It's a physical law of balance. But most people translate physical laws to emotional and spiritual laws. From that comparison we begin to believe that if I give you love, than now you have more love and I have less love. But that doesn't ring true. In fact, the opposite is how it is truly experienced. When I give love and you receive love I now have the experience of reinforcing what I already have and possess. We cannot give what we do not have. So if I am giving love I am reinforcing the experience of actually having it. The same is true for our gifts and medicine. To experience having them, we must give them. We must live as though that medicine is already in us.

Too often we are taught to compete and that in order to be significant, we must win and outshine others. But if we begin to shift our perspective to the foundation that our fire within is unique to each and every one of us, then there becomes no need to compete and withhold that which is uniquely internal. There would be enough for everyone to win, to shine, to partake in processes and projects that serve the whole, rather than the individual. To compete and withhold our gifts with others is a context of scarcity and "not enough-ness" that leaves everyone lacking and living under full potential. The mistruth that if we are to give what we have, then that would mean that we lose what we give away. Luckily, this is not how spiritual and emotional laws work. These laws are not based in scarcity, but rather in the abundance of universal and natural laws.

For years I fought the Medicine in me. I tried to run from it and delay it. I was certain I wasn't ready to embrace it. Since I was young, I have always related to and revered Native American wisdom. The philosophies of balance, interconnectedness with nature and all of life resonated deep inside my soul. I have deep respect for all religions and walks of life but the ceremonies and practices of our Native people are the framework of my spiritual practice. For years I felt reluctant to share my principles and findings of inner peace that I was able to cultivate and live by. Through a series of failures, misfortunes and self-inflicted mess-ups, finally I realized that denying the medicine in me was actually causing me suffering.

I remember going through a time of struggle and serendipitously meeting a shaman and telling him of my youth when I carved my first chanunpa, a sacred pipe, (many people know it as a peace pipe) and I learned the sacred pipe ceremony when I was 17. For years I kept it to myself, not allowing others to partake in the ceremony for fear that I would seem strange. He simply said to me, "Son, if you are carving a pipe at 17, you didn't find the pipe, the sacred pipe found you." I was blessed and honored to have such practices so close to my heart and soul that it was ultimately time to give them away and contribute them. To honor the gifts that were put in my heart became a sacred blessing to me and ever since the moment I have embraced them and incorporated them into my practices and purpose of healing, my life has been forever changed.

As we connect to our medicine, own it and give it, we begin to create a life that is rooted in principle, honor, authenticity and fulfillment. We build an inner framework that has us trust ourselves and our gifts and give them freely while reinforcing the very nature of abundance within us. To withhold our medicine and to stay lost behind confusion and doubt it, is to delay and sell our lives short and live a life of mediocrity, at best. The New Man Emerging taps into his uniqueness, he lives it and protects it like a warrior guarding a village. He knows that it is worth defending with all of his heart.

NME Exercise:

To get clear on your Purpose and your Medicine spend 20 mins each day in silence. Get comfortable in a seated position and connect with your breath. As you get grounded, simply ask these questions...

1) *What is the experience I crave in my life?*
2) *What unique gifts have I been given?*
3) *What would I be willing to die for?*
4) *How can I best serve others?*

Each day journal what is revealed to you and start over fresh the next day until you get clear in your heart. Notice what patterns you see and be completely honest with yourself.

CHANNEL YOUR CREATIVITY

After we connect, own and give our medicine we begin to live from a place of meaning and purpose. We start to see that as we give from a genuine place that we are filled up even as we are giving. We develop practices and business that are not only creative and fun but also fulfilling and aligned to a higher and deeper purpose within us. Do not be surprised that as you dive deeper into your passion and inner fire that ideas, insights, projects and desires begin to reveal themselves to you. Life can shift in a moment from drab and predictable to exciting and meaningful, the moment you are truly willing to see your existence from a new perspective.

A commitment to transformation brings an influx of revelation and meaning and often times it becomes challenging to home in on what it is that you desire to create. Many men will want to take on multiple roles and try to wear many hats. They will start several business or projects at once or try to transform too many things in their life all at the same time. It is a shame when men have great ideas but don't know how to bring them to life.

We are taught that knowledge is power. Knowledge is not power, knowledge is potential power. Knowledge with committed action is power. We must take our ideas from a creative phase to an action phase or else we will die with brilliant ideas that never came to life. Just as the seasons have distinct weather, so too do the energies of our life. We must distinguish the use of energy for where we are at with our dreams, visions and projects so that we can give them and give them effectively.

As we get clear and trust our medicine, in the phase of giving it we must be vigilant about the energy we use and harness. We must dress for the season, so to speak, so that we are utilizing our focuses with purpose. Whether we are starting a business, fueling a new habit or cultivating new relationships, we must understand that to bring any new vision to life there are 3 phases and they must be handled with mindfulness so that they are able to come to fruition.

Phase 1 - Innovate

The first phase of bringing our vision to life is the phase of innovation. This is the idea phase, vision phase. This is where we discover our big "why"; the reason we do what we do and why we want to bring our medicine to life. This is the phase that demands clarity through exploration. Our goal is to discover what it is that truly would be worth bringing to life. When we live purposefully, it must be for something greater than simply our own needs, pleasures or profits. For true fulfillment and meaning, we must serve something greater than us. In this phase of discovery, it is vital to ask 2 important questions...

Who do I wish to serve?
How do I serve them?

Who does your medicine serve? What is the unique gift that you have and by bringing it to life who benefits by it? This is a vital question because too often a good-hearted man will want to answer that they "wish to serve everyone." This is actually quite dangerous because these are the men that typically end up serving no one or just a few. Their medicine becomes diluted because it lacks the potency that is needed to cut to the core of the heart of those that seek to learn, benefit and grow from their uniqueness. Instead of reaching everyone, his message and medicine reaches no one. And they are left exhausted and disheartened, not due to lack of effort but due to lack of response.

93

It wreaks havoc on the spirit when our medicine goes unnoticed and unappreciated. However, it is on us to get clear on the message that we offer and to deliver it in such a way that it is clear, concise and honest in our work, relationships and life. We must commit to discover, to innovate, and to create something unique and new that solves a frustration for those around us. This is to live with purpose and to serve, a vital component to the New Man Emerging.

After we see whom it is we wish to serve, we then must ask ourselves, "how?" what is the platform that we will create, innovate and make new? What is the voice piece that we will use to message our hearts and how will we give it? What platform is most effective for lifting others up and also marrying your passions with your profits? Money is not the root of all evil, greed is. The New Man Emerging knows that by being clear that his purpose is to serve others and choose a platform that is poignant and direct, he understands that greed is not his motive, service is.

In this day and age, there are so many platforms that have leveled the playing field for the everyday man. Long gone are the days when exorbitant capital was needed to buy storefronts and start endeavors. Now, with the Internet, self-publishing, blogging, online marketing etc. the game has changed dramatically in recent years. The way we gather and connect is evolving. But we must not let these platforms evolve past creating value, meaning and purpose. Connect to your medicine, realize whom it serves, find the platform to deliver it and guarantee that value and meaning are at its core.

Phase 2 - Generate

After we get clear on our ideas in the innovation phase we must step into phase 2, generate. This is the phase of action that I call "warrior mode." This is head down, hit the ground running and make it happen. Too many people stop with ideas and fail to launch their visions into reality for fear of failure and ridicule. In the generate phase we must welcome failure. This is the phase that we test, attempt, mess up and learn. One of my mentors constantly reminds me "There is no failure, there is only feedback." Therefore we either succeed or learn.

In this phase, we must add committed action and continue to grow and learn. This is the phase of the majority of our growth. For instance, if we are starting a business that we are passionate about, this will be the area we make our attempts to launch it, get it off the ground and make small, subtle adjustments over time that have it grow and become prosperous. Too many people want to jump from idea to CEO and bypass the hard work that it takes to get there. They lack patience, persistence and the audacity to see further than the average person's reasonableness. Where most stop, the New Man Emerging must press on.

This phase requires action and hard work. It demands of us consistency and determination to give even the smallest details our attention. What are you innovating; a business, a relationship, your health? Whatever it is, it will require of you to push forward, to reshape yourself beyond your comfort zone and your familiarity. Whatever it is that you are innovating is new. That means you do not know the road ahead except through your willingness to try, learn and grow. It is a new creation but it will die without your consistency to fuel it and nurture it through your commitment. The certainty ahead is only fueled by your actions in this moment. So often we want a giant spotlight projected on our future ahead and yet the best we are given is a flashlight that simply shines on the next step.

The generate phase is masculine. It is fueled by determination that leads to freedom. Can you access that part of you that is immovable and steadfast, so that your vision goes from ethereal to tangible? You must be cautious here to not allow yourself to become distracted, adding in new ideas before you have tested the initial one that you have committed to. If you fail to stay committed, you will get distracted by greener grass and dilute your efforts in too many places rather than tend to the grass where you stand.

Most people stop with ideas, the rest stop here. This phase will test your wholehearted commitment. To quit before you succeed is to let the fire in you fade. In Napoleon Hill's classic book, "Think and Grow Rich," he tells the story of the uncle of R.U. Darby who travels to Colorado during the Gold Rush. He initially strikes a little bit of fortune, but when it seems to run dry, he quits. He then sells his tools to a junk man who goes back to the same mine, and after digging for only 3 feet, he strikes a fortune. R.U. Darby's uncle literally quit 3 feet from gold!

In the generate phase it is important to be present. Many people miss the nuances of success and think that it 100% or nothing; A+ or F. Success is subtle and it grows with every committed action and attempt. Rather than only see the end, we must be present to the subtleties along the way. It is important in this phase to ask certain questions so that you can monitor your trend and progress. The most important questions along the way are these ...

What is working?

What is in the way?

What is one shift I can make to have success next time?

Even if you haven't reached the desired destination, you can still see what states worked. It is valuable to focus on what is working while you are pursuing your goals. If you constantly focus on what is not working it will be too easy in the generate phase to want to abandon your commitment and go back to the innovate phase where it tends to be more exciting. Continue to focus on what is working and polish it constantly.

It is also incredibly useful to ask yourself and your team, "What is in the way?" Often times here it is easy to see circumstances that are challenging and blame them for lack of success. But where we really want to point to is a place of personal responsibility. If conditions don't change, how can you adjust yourself to still have it happen? Remember, average people run their lives based on their circumstances, extraordinary people run their lives based on their commitments. In the generate phase, you want to be constantly inner reflective on your states of being to see where you are withholding and what next level you still get to bring your gifts to, in order to reach new growth and expansion.

Finally, you want to make one shift after each new attempt. Don't abandon everything and make your next attempt totally new. Simply adjust one thing and make small shifts each time. Keep what works, leave what doesn't. Only take with you what is useful. With this approach not only will you be able to achieve success but you will also be able to duplicate it. That is what is most important.

Sustainable success is in the details. It is vital to pause along the journey of success and debrief your outcomes and results while celebrating the small wins and learning from any shortcomings. I love watching infants learn to walk. They stand up, fall down and then try again. But what we don't see is that every time they attempt to walk and make a new effort, their brain receives a new message. And each time they try, they adjust their next attempt by just a hair. And finally, they walk.

It takes countless attempts for toddlers to learn to walk. And yet, as adults, we try something we care about once or twice and if it doesn't work we abandon it. The fear of ridicule and failure has most people trapped from even attempting what they truly desire.

If you are courageous enough to have moved to this phase of your creative process you still have one phase to go. If you stop here you become a slave to your own creation. You won't be able to step away from it or it will begin to require so much of your time and energy that you will become resentful of it. I have heard so many men tell me that they always wanted to "do their own thing" and now that they are they feel trapped by it. It becomes like Frankenstein in a sense and now it owns you. This is due to one simple correction ... We always want to generate with a purpose, and the purpose is always the same ...

Phase 3 - Automate

When we generate we want to be aimed at something. If we are not, then our hard work becomes painstaking and fruitless. The end goal of a vision or project is always the same, to automate or sustain our vision. This means that we want to get it to a point that it runs naturally on its own without much involvement from you; so that it is brainless or can be easily duplicated. If it is a business, we want to build it in such a way that you can step away from it when needed. This means having the best possible team in place and systems that are always aimed at your freedom. If this is a habit or action, then this is the point where it is on automatic and is now naturally built into your lifestyle. The time and energy it takes in innovation and generation mode are consuming but this is the phase that makes it all worth it.

The importance of automating and sustaining your visions, goals and projects is critical. Too often people try to do too many things at once and none of them come to fruition. It is not a lack of effort or even energy; it is a lack of sequence and effectively channeling creativity. If we have too many projects and commitments, none of them will receive our proper attention that they deserve, and life will constantly feel like a juggling act or the things we desire to achieve will never make it to fruition. When things are sustained and automated, they are advancing with little effort from us, and that frees our energy up to innovate something new that is important to us.

At one point, this book was an innovation. It was simply an idea. It stayed an idea for a long time until I finally shifted into the generate phase. Writing day in, day out. Warrior mode. Over time, and through committed action, it came together. The moment it was completed, it then became automated; available for distribution and sale without much effort from me. While it travels on its own, I am already onto my next innovation.

The challenge for most men is that they want to do too much at once. This becomes a trap. Rather than focus our effort and creativity on one thing at a time we get distracted and try to build too much too fast. When we choose one thing, focus our energy on what is most important, we can see it to fruition and then allow it to become automatically operational. Then, we can move on to the next passion or project knowing that what we've created now only needs a little effort and attention from us.

The goal is to make things habitual or automatic. If we have to think too much about every domain in our life, eventually we begin to abandon our successful protocols and procedures. To lose weight is one thing, but to lose weight and keep it off by a sustained and automated process of a lifestyle is something else entirely. We want to build in brainless and automated rituals that generate continued success. This is far easier done one-at-a-time. Get your goals to automatic by instilling the effective systems in place for your life's success.

Once you feel you have automated and sustained your current innovation, then the question is always "What do I want to innovate next?" Since you have made things habitual you will be able to add new innovations on top of a successful foundation of growth. This is the recipe that allows us to focus and channel our creativity so that it is effective and easily maintained. If you have too many innovations happening at once that aren't on a solid foundation, then chances of sustained success are minimal.

For the New Man Emerging, freedom is his ultimate goal. If he is trapped by his own makings he will never achieve full potential. We must see where our creativities are being fueled and supported and where we are trapping ourselves due to overextension. Innovate, generate, automate and watch as your creativity becomes ignited and properly channeled to a life of passion and fulfillment.

NME Exercise:

Audit your creativities. List out the creative intentions that you have always wanted to achieve. After doing so, section them to NOW, LATER or NO LONGER WANT. Notice where you are channeling energy into what you no longer want and free up that energy for what you want now. Innovate that, one thing at a time. As you bring it to sustainable and automated then revisit your "LATER" column and innovate the next thing from there.

WHAT IS IT ALL FOR?

"No price is too high to pay for the privilege of owning yourself."
— Rudyard Kipling

Human beings are creatures of value. In all we do, there is at least a perceived value in it. If you think you do anything in life without getting something for it, then you are kidding yourself. In all our actions, moods, behaviors and choices there must be some value that we perceive at the end of it to for us to carry it through. Those end values and payoffs are not always healthy but they are there, do not fool yourself. Often times they are the payoffs of security, attention, comfort, familiarity, significance etc. These payoffs and values are often unconscious in the minds of human beings and the patterns associated with them have been practiced for so long that they feel unbreakable.

We forget that the value attached to the end of a thought system and behavior keeps unhealthy patterns and habits rooted in our lives and in our psyche. The New Man Emerging seeks to not only unlock and discover these unhealthy patterns but to blast them wide open at their core and replace them with payoffs and values that serve him and all those he loves.

Because human beings are creatures of value, it is not uncommon or dishonest to ask the question, "What's in it for me?" At the root of all behaviors this question is there so we might as well be honest about it. This doesn't make men selfish; it simply points to the underlying need of significance that we all seek to have in our lives. Awakening in consciousness has the question become more connected to healthy payoffs and values and evolves naturally from "What's in it for me?" to "How best can I serve?"

"How best can I serve life, my woman (or man), my family, my community and the world?"

The evolving man is clear about what he gains from this journey of self-discovery, of awareness and consciousness and living a life of principle and value. The payoff is simply this; he gets to be "a man in possession of himself." No longer ruled and run by reactive behaviors of the past, unconscious limiting belief systems and triggered by the wounds of yesterday, he is present, in possession of his thinking, behaviors and actions and his love is poignant and direct. He is unmovable and unwavering as a mountain in a storm to his values and principles as a man. This comes not from a place of righteousness and opposition, but from a place of clarity of vision; clear, honest, direct, present and dignified.

To be a man in possession of your self is to know who you are at your core. Beyond the labels of what society has placed on you, beyond what mom and dad have told you or expected of you, beyond your reflex to please everyone or rebel against the system, you stand firm in your heart and mind because you have done the work, you've let the fire of self-inquiry burn away the labels of identity that you clung to for decades and you have taken the axe to your own limited roots of unworthiness. And you survived, you succeeded. And you lived to tell of the journey of your becoming. Now as you face the world of men and woman you can stand confident and firm in the presence of whom you are beyond the labels and the naming of things. You are present, whole, complete, enough.

In the Lakota Sioux Tribes of the plains of North America, they had a term called "*wica*". Wica was a "complete man." It was what every Lakota boy strived to be. According to Joseph M. Marshall III in his book The Journey of Crazy Horse, he writes, "Wica was the kind of man who demonstrated the highest Lakota virtues of generosity, courage, fortitude and wisdom." These are inner states that men possess, but they must be practiced, honed, tempered and called forth. The payoffs for accessing and making these states valued beyond others are confidence, leadership and self-esteem. Our current culture teaches us that we must acquire these states by our accomplishments, achievements and acquisitions. Hence, men are lost, constantly searching for identity outside of themselves in things and status. It is a fruitless journey that leaves men depleted, frustrated and jaded.

The journey we are pointing to is an inward journey of remembering; a discovery that what we thought was lost was simply hidden. There is an understanding that esteem and worth were never lacking but covered by the labels that were sold and bought by a culture that was desperately looking for itself. And now we are realizing that those states can never be found in a world of temporary and transient things. Rather they are to be called forth from within, to be in possession of and to be honed, honored and sharpened like the sword of the fiercest warrior.

This is what all of it is for, this is what the New Man Emerging gains; the ability to walk into the world and be led by his inner state rather than the noise of the confused chatter that surrounds him. It is to be part of society without being owned by it; undistracted by its latest trends or swept up into its latest hysterias. It is to live a life that is fueled by purpose rather than possessions. His experience of inner character is held more valuable than the climbing of an imaginary ladder of false identities and success.

Let me be clear, there is nothing wrong with possessions, accumulations or status but if it runs you rather than you possess it, it will have you and control you until the day you die. Let what you own be an expression of your inner states rather than a definition of them. The things you accomplish or accumulate will never fill the gaps of self-worth and fulfillment until you yourself own your inner world. We see this time and again with people reaching pinnacles of success only to take their own life and be haunted by the belief of "not enough-ness."

To be in possession of your self is to own your inner world; every corner of it. You have willingly shone a light on all your shadows and met them as the illusions that they are. They are not you, but simply a part of you that required healing. It is to have failed and met failure with the same enthusiasm as your triumphs and learned from them just the same and remained confident and humble in either outcome. It is to pursue the experiences of life, the highs and lows of joy and sorrows rather than chase the perfect identity to wear that will have you save face and fool your fellow brothers and sisters with pretenses. Your life is not designed to be figured out, it is designed to be experienced and lived; all of it, fully. And the greatest tools you have to live deeply and passionately come from your ability to own your inner world and that which you already possess.

WELCOME THE WAR WITHIN

Your inner possession and wholeness, requires all of you, not just the parts you like and admire. Too often, we default to our strengths and ignore our blind spots and shadows. To be a man in possession of himself you must own all the parts of you, even the ones you would rather ignore or run from. Joy comes from being fully self-expressed, but so often we want to only own the "good" parts of our character and personalities rather than embrace the whole of us, blemishes and all. This reluctance and resistance has us become imbalanced like a foundation that only has a few healthy pillars.

We must be willing to shine the light on our souls to truly illuminate for ourselves the inner workings that are required to live a deep, fulfilling and authentic life. To run from our demons is to delay our possibilities and stunt our potential. We must be true to our inner fire, which is fueled by both the yin and yang of who we are. We are so commonly taught as men to hide, suppress or pretend that we are bothered by nothing and be some kind of emotionless rock that feels or experiences no pain. This is childish, foolish and dangerous. We are taught to run from our demons, pretend we are more than something we are not and to overcompensate for our flaws. Instead we hide what it is that we truly desire and punish ourselves for actually desiring it. Rather, we must look within our own hearts and minds and welcome the war within.

Welcoming the war within is to own up to, with complete honesty, where we feel our life is lacking and then take complete ownership of all our outcomes. To welcome the war is to be willing to dive into our deepest desires and admit where we experience guilt, scarcity and unworthiness. It is to turn the mirror on ourselves and claim that nothing externally can draw forth our inner state without our will. No man, woman or the world can rob us of our peace without our allowing them to do so.

The war is our victimhood, our belief in scarcity and our succumbing to fear. It is the place in our heart that we have allowed doubt and fear to fester like a virus, unwilling to address it. And we allow it to spread like a cancer throughout the host body of our life. Through guilt and shame we try to override our fears hoping that one day they will evaporate and handle themselves, but they don't and they won't. We must access courage, willingness and earnestness to truly look deep within ourselves and own every limitation that we experience in our lives.

The war within feels like an inner scramble. It is uncomfortable at first. It is the feeling of uneasiness that comes from a deep-rooted fear of being abandoned or losing love and affection. Because we are not effectively taught and mentored by the generations before us on how to handle the inner turmoil in a healthy way, our typical solutions are usually to numb and suppress it with compulsion or addiction. This can be substance abuse such as alcohol and drugs, as well as gambling and pornography. It can also be an addiction to people's approval, affection, looking good in the eyes of others and needing everyone to like you. These are traps set forth by the limited mind that will never be satisfied because it is built on the perception of lack. We numb out the discomfort only to welcome it again with the next failure, compulsion or fix. It is a vicious cycle that we create. We are trapped by our own belief system of scarcity and unworthiness. "If only I got everyone to like me,' 'If only I do everything right,' 'If only I could just get X,Y & Z...'" "Then I will be happy and satisfied." We do this only to notice that the fix wears off and we are left feeling even emptier than before. So, we try harder, do it better, scream louder, force more, only to leave ourselves depleted and unfulfilled. And the only payoff we receive is the continued belief that we are guilty and unworthy, landing in the very same place we started.

To be truly free, we must welcome the war within us. The split mind of where we think we cannot access emotion, feelings and desires. A man must learn how to live with a broken heart. And rather than let it paralyze him, use the cracks and tears to gain access to the doorway of his soul. We must invite it in and access the courage to meet it straight on, face to face.

To heal the split mind of fear, we must see it for what it truly is, the demon and making of our own minds. We must welcome the war, we must rise up to the challenge that it calls forth from within us, and at the moment we seek to slay it, we must set down our swords and walk off the battlefield completely. This is a concept that my brother Christopher teaches in a course he wrote called The Masculine Journey. That the war will never be won in our mind; it will only be won in our heart. It will never be won in the mind because it was created by the mind in the first place. It is like a knife that can cut one thousand things but no matter what, it will never be able to cut itself. Same with the war in the mind. It created a narrative that you are not good enough, that you are separate from each other and the rest of life and that you will always have to fight. But in the fight the war stays waged and the fearful mind continues to live on.

It is time, as men, that we welcome the war and that we do the work necessary to heal all our past wounds that have us cut off from our women, our world and ourselves. The heart of a man will be his savior if he has the courage to connect it with his disciplined mind. No emotion will kill us. No past action is unforgiveable and no limiting belief can hide the light of who you are forever. It is time; time to accept all the facets of yourself, your being and your truth. To accept it is to allow it the space to move inside you and eventually let nature do its healing work. The scramble will heal you. But you must allow it to do so. No running, no hiding, no pretending. If you have past traumas and life defining events that require extra work on your part, do not wait and hesitate to discover the modalities that will benefit you in your recovery to your full self. Trauma work, groups, transformational trainings, breath work, shamanic practices, spiritual work and mentorships to name a few are all avenues that have us connect to our growth through our past limitations. Do not wait; time does not heal all wounds. Time well spent does.

We must remind each other, our boys and ourselves that having emotions and feelings is not weak or wrong but rather natural and human. They are a part of who we are and must be felt and expressed. Being half of ourselves will not suffice. We must be complete and whole, and express each part of who we are, to be fulfilled, powerful and free. It is through our willingness and embracing who we are, including all aspects of our self that we will become whole again and live as free men.

BE HER HERO

If you are not her hero, then you are wasting her time. A man must be the hero in his own story. This is the journey of becoming, the journey of the New Man Emerging. The journey reshapes us and calls forth our honor, integrity, challenges our principles and gives us opportunities to practice what we say is important to us in our inner and outer worlds. Every day we have the opportunity to make a mark and leave our dent in infinity. And one of our greatest vehicles to do so is in our relationships.

As a man becomes the hero in his own story he inevitably becomes hers too. (This applies to gay couples as well.) To live a life in accordance with purpose and principle will be the barometer on which we gauge our depth of effectiveness in the world. Your woman's feedback, insight and states will give you a unique perspective into how you are showing up as a man in life. Let us be clear, this is not a call to acquiesce and pander to your woman's every desire. This is an invitation to live a life congruent to your uniqueness and qualities that make you distinct in the world. And because of that commitment, you allow your relationship and woman's love to get caught up in the wake of your purpose, vision and fulfillment. This is an invitation to allow her to nurture your growth, challenge your blind spots and test the very core of which you are, so that you emerge the hero in your and her story. Anything less would be a waste of time for you both.

The most common trip-up here is that many men collapse pressing forward in vision to pleasing people. As you move forward through your challenges of awakening, you may not, most likely will not, please everyone. This is a huge hurdle to overcome for many men. Many men stop at the idea that this is going to make people uncomfortable, that this conversation may be tough or that he doesn't want to hear his woman's displeasure. So, he stops; sometimes before he begins. And he is left feeling regretful and resentful. Rather than seeing the possibility that the end of her displeasure can be the start of her joy and he sees through on his commitments, no matter how challenging or interruptive his vision may be.

In the process of evolving, we allow the journey to shape us and to call forth the very states we say are important to us. Life will forever give us the ground in which to test our growth and challenge what we give our mind, hearts and word to. This journey of becoming is what Joseph Campbell coined "The Hero's Journey." This journey of returning home, to purity, to wholeness is the greatest journey any of us could ever choose.

As you allow the journey to shape you, you inevitably become the hero in the foreground of your story. Let her see that. Let her nurture your growth and challenge your blind spots so that in your failures there are seeds of wisdom. This is a call beyond mere accomplishments and the false idea that one day when you attain or achieve "X", then you have arrived. You won't, there is no end mountaintop and as long as you are wearing skin there is another level for you. As you dedicate your life to the journey that demands all you have to give and offer, she will see it, be drawn to it and love you for it, even in her testing. If she doesn't, she's not the one for you and you are not the one for her. And you can both move on. Your task is to explore your inner world and forge a purpose in your life from the inside out that you and your partner are proud of and live with meaning. Anything less than that and you are withholding on her and she will know it. She deserves all that you have; the giver, the protector, the lover and the sage. All of you. And when you confidently stand in who you are, she will know it. And she will fuel you forward greater than any propeller in the world.

The New Man Emerging has his mission and purpose at the foreground of his life. Work, accomplishments and even his relationships are not his end goal; they are platforms and vehicles in which he has to express his deepest form of loving. His woman (or man) is not his possession or conquest, but rather the physical form and vessel in which to pour his love. He doesn't look to his woman for fulfillment because fulfillment is his ultimate aim in life and his cup is his alone to fill. She receives all that runs over. He is also not lost in her moods, trying to fix her emotional states, analyze her defects or tolerate her until she "gets over it." Instead, he loves her, in this moment, as she is; without trying to fix her or advance her to a new moment. He is present. Unmoved. Committed to love and her feeling it through his eyes and his open heart. He does not run, he does not pander. He breathes deeply, stays present and blankets her with an intense love that could pierce the walls of her heart that she thought she needed to protect. And then she is back to loving, all herself. His woman's praise is welcomed but not needed. His honor and principles are the standard which he lives. And his woman is his greatest reminder, test and barometer.

She wants all of you. Here and now. She will love you greater than you can imagine but that will require you to move through your karma, your past hurts and all the wounds left by mom and dad. She wants you, not the broken boy in you. The inner work dedicated to moving through the past is as intense as it is necessary. But you will be present to love. You will see her in the moment and not the past heartbreaks of the women that cheated you emotionally and left you jaded. Your justifications of why it isn't safe to love won't work on her over time. She demands all of you in this moment. And she deserves it. Anything less and she will let you know in her subtle, and sometimes not so subtle, ways.

Whenever possible, know your purpose first, then find your woman. If a man doesn't know his deepest mission in life he will always be left feeling empty or falling short. He won't be able to show up to work and woman and family in his fullest because the deepest part of him is actually missing and lost. When a man knows his mission and aim in life he is able to show up fully to all moments because his life is aligned to that ultimate goal of freedom and fulfillment. If you choose your women before your purpose you will get lost and distracted from a life that is half empty and constantly trying to fill it with temporary pleasures and fixes. Remember, the nagging will never go away and if you are distracted from your purpose in life, it will feel further and further away each year until you wake one day and wonder how you got to where you are. Forge your purpose and then find the woman that will feed it.

If you are with her now, be her hero. The day she said "I do" was not the day your work ended; it was the day your work began. If you haven't been her hero then be honest and start immediately. Be the man that you would want your daughter to marry. Reshape and shift your life so that your principles enter the room before you, so deeply and committed that your woman knows it. She will love you because she trusts you. Trusts that you will not waiver from your deepest truth just to please her or please the world. She will test you and if you are evolving and committed to your own awakening, you will thank her. You will not want it or her any other way.

"If you want to change the world... love a woman-really love her.
Find the one who calls to your soul, who doesn't make sense.
Throw away your check list and put your ear to her heart and listen.
Hear the names, the prayers, the songs of every living thing-
every winged one, every furry and scaled one,
every underground and underwater one, every green and flowering one,
every not yet born and dying one...
Hear their melancholy praises back to the One who gave them life.
If you haven't heard your own name yet, you haven't listened long enough.
If your eyes aren't filled with tears, if you aren't bowing at her feet,
you haven't ever grieved having almost lost her.

If you want to change the world... love a woman-one woman
beyond yourself, beyond desire and reason,
beyond your male preferences for youth, beauty and variety

and all your superficial concepts of freedom.
We have given ourselves so many choices
we have forgotten that true liberation
comes from standing in the middle of the soul's fire
and burning through our resistance to Love.
There is only one Goddess.
Look into Her eyes and see-really see
if she is the one to bring the axe to your head.
If not, walk away. Right now.
Don't waste time "trying."
Know that your decision has nothing to do with her
because ultimately, it's not with who,
but when we choose to surrender.

If you want to change the world ... love a woman.
Love her for life-beyond your fear of death,
beyond your fear of being manipulated
by the Mother inside your head.
Don't tell her you're willing to die for her.
Say you're willing to LIVE with her,
plant trees with her and watch them grow.
Be her hero by telling her how beautiful she is in her vulnerable majesty,
by helping her to remember every day that she IS Goddess
through your adoration and devotion.

If you want to change the world ... love a woman
in all her faces, through all her seasons
and she will heal you of your schizophrenia-
your double-mindedness and half-heartedness
which keeps your Spirit and body separate-
which keeps you alone and always looking outside your Self
for something to make your life worth living.
There will always be another woman.
Soon the new shiny one will become the old dull one
and you'll grow restless again, trading in women like cars,

trading in the Goddess for the latest object of your desire.
Man doesn't need any more choices.
What man needs is Woman, the Way of the Feminine,
of Patience and Compassion, non-seeking, non-doing,
of breathing in one place and sinking deep intertwining roots
strong enough to hold the Earth together
while she shakes off the cement and steel from her skin.

If you want to change the world … love a woman, just one woman .
Love and protect her as if she is the last holy vessel.
Love her through her fear of abandonment
which she has been holding for all of humanity.
No, the wound is not hers to heal alone.
No, she is not weak in her codependence.

If you want to change the world … love a woman
all the way through
until she believes you,
until her instincts, her visions, her voice, her art, her passion,
her wildness have returned to her-
until she is a force of love more powerful
than all the political media demons who seek to devalue and destroy her.

If you want to change the world,
lay down your causes, your guns and protest signs.
Lay down your inner war, your righteous anger
and love a woman …
beyond all of your striving for greatness,
beyond your tenacious quest for enlightenment.
The holy grail stands before you
if you would only take her in your arms
and let go of searching for something beyond this intimacy.

What if peace is a dream which can only be re-membered
through the heart of Woman?

What if a man's love for Woman, the Way of the Feminine
is the key to opening Her heart?

If you want to change the world... love a woman
to the depths of your shadow,
to the highest reaches of your Being,
back to the Garden where you first met her,
to the gateway of the rainbow realm
where you walk through together as Light as One,
to the point of no return,
to the ends and the beginning of a new Earth."

— Lisa Citore

As I stated earlier, my mistakes and blind spots are far too many to count. In the arena of "Being Her Hero" I have tried, failed and tried again. My old patterns of pleasing people, telling half-truths to be liked and falling for women that I could fix so that deep down I would feel a sense of worth, are all too common in my past. Seeing it now, I know that I, like others, have left a wake of emotional collateral damage behind. For this I am sorry to anyone that was ever hurt. But I have learned. I have learned to look within myself and clear a space so that love can emerge; that all the blocks of unworthiness and shame I placed there, were just shadows and illusions that I myself cast. Over time I made them real, but they never were. The work that it has taken me to return to my innocence and self-love has been a steep and arduous climb, but worth every step.

Today, there are no words that my woman can say to me that are sweeter than the words "You are my hero." No "I love yous" that can touch my core more tenderly than that of how she truly sees me as the hero of her world. Those words are music and after hearing them I feel I can conquer any challenge. I do not go to her to have my cup filled but rather go to her to pour my love into her, and in the process she loves me and reminds me my cup is even bigger than I had known. Her love is beyond measure and words and her love fuels my mission in life greater than any fire.

To be her hero is to know in the depths of your heart with certainty that no one can love her better than you. If someone can, you must let her go to find him. To be her hero is to give her all that you are in your heart and mind that is aligned to your gifts and mission and allow her to fuel your mission with a depth of love that is unattainable on your own. To live with honor, to make your life one of purpose and for her to be the ultimate recipient of your love will stimulate your growth to a potential that currently may escape you. Anything else is a waste of time.

FOUNDATIONS FOR FULFILLMENT

O ne of the greatest confusions and mix ups that I see with most men and their lack of happiness comes from confusing success with fulfillment. This has been an incredible modern day trap that I see repeated constantly. The assumption is that if a man is successful in one domain of his life such as career, then that success will inevitably overflow into other domains of his life like relationships. It is simply untrue as well as ineffective. I have coached countless men who are successful in business or career, while at the same time their health or marriage is suffering.

It is typical to see someone get to a pinnacle of accomplishment of life and look back and see collateral damage of health, relationships or fulfillment. This is simply because success and fulfillment are not the same thing. How many men have made it to the mountaintops of achievement and lost their health along the way? Or who has gained status and accomplishment only to have their wife be unhappy and their marriages implode along their journey to the "top?" It happens far too often because we were taught to over-focus on building success (typically for men it is in the work domain) and never paid enough attention to the other foundational aspects of life that build fulfillment over time. We make money but then have no leisure time to actually use it for the things we love and enjoy doing. We go to jobs that stress us out and complain that there is not enough time to build a spiritual practice or look after our health. We go months, sometimes years, without speaking or connecting to the people we truly care about and they often don't realize how important they are to us. When we chase success without the framework of fulfillment then our happiness will become fleeting at best, and we will be left cleaning up the unintentional damage that we unconsciously caused along our way.

The domains of our lives are foundational. Meaning we build our lives upon them and they support us in all our endeavors for happiness and fulfillment. When one foundation suffers, the whole structure suffers. It is of no use to have one solid foundation in your home and the rest be broken. When one leg is healthy and the other injured, the whole body is affected. One leg doesn't rejoice at the other legs misfortune. The same holds true with our lives. We have domains that are foundational to our fulfillment. Typical domains include, but aren't limited to ...

Career - Relationship - Health - Relationship(s) - Leisure - Spiritual Life - Community

Let us define these domains or foundations as the areas of our lives that require and deserve an appropriate amount of our love and attention. Notice the distinction "appropriate" amount of love and attention. They all deserve love and attention but there are seasons of our lives where one may require a bit more than the other. There may be times in life where work or a new project requires more love and attention than your leisure life or other times when your marriage requires more love and attention than your work. You must be discerning on where it is that you are devoting your commodities. The trick is to feed, fuel and build all your domains up without it being at the expense of other domains. There is no sense in advancing one foundation while one or another domain suffers. It will cause unbalance in life or the constant feeling of overwhelm or that there are just too many balls in the air to juggle.

One of the greatest mistakes that people make is to over-focus their love and attention on just one domain. They will put everything they have into, let's say work, all the while leaving no time to focus on the other building blocks of their life. They overcommit or spend all their energy day in and day out only to come home and have no energy for their loved ones, leisure life or health. If this goes on for too long they will wake up one day in a form of "mid-life crisis" and wonder where all their time went. They will look around and see that they "missed it;" time with their families, passions, and service to their communities and wonder how it got to this place. This is because we have been taught to over focus on one domain and then have been falsely promised that that domain will spill into others.

I hear so often that men who are successful in their business don't understand why their family life is struggling. To which, ironically, their solution is to simply work harder. This won't work. The love and attention that your business requires is not the same love and attention that your family requires and deserves. They are distinct. And if you cannot distinguish between them, your fulfillment will suffer. Working more or harder won't fix your marriage. Procrastinating in addressing your health to constantly meet work goals will never add to your vitality and in the long run will dramatically deplete it.

The New Man Emerging knows how to distinguish and discern what energy goes where. He understands that his power is in his presence; that to choose to be here and now with his domains is all that is important in this moment. We see constantly in our culture of hurry that people are together but their minds are somewhere else. That they can be sitting together at restaurants but on their phones fantasizing about the next moment, lacking presence of here and now. People are perceptive. They know when you are not truly present with them. They know when you are not listening and paying attention, especially your spouse. If your mind is constantly obsessed with one domain of your life, you will begin to weaken others and the fulfillment that you could experience in life will be impossible.

> *"It is of no use walking anywhere to preach*
> *unless our walking is our preaching."*
> — St Francis of Assisi

We must begin to practice presence. To choose to be here and now. The greatest places to practice are the domains of our lives, the areas that require an appropriate amount of love and attention. All of our domains require it, some more than others at different phases and seasons of our lives. Though they all must receive it without harming the others. To truly create fulfillment in our lives we must undo the conditioning that success in one area leads to fulfillment in all others. It is simply not true. Instead, we must get present to what matters to us and begin to shift our energy so that all domains are met with the appropriate amount of love and attention. Here's the trick…

It is better to advance all the domains of your life by one inch than one domain of your life by one mile.
— *Gary Grant*

Read that line again if you must because it is the very foundation of fulfillment. Unless everything you value is touched and blessed by you, it will atrophy and wither. All the domains of our lives require our presence. They must be sustained and lifted to a place that it becomes habitual for us that they get our gifts and our concentration. Anything less will be a disservice to them and to ourselves. It is unwise to believe that the things we love and value will handle themselves and simply work out in our life by fate or luck. That which we value in our life requires our full participation. Nothing great will come to you without your willingness to be its full generator. Ignoring anything that is important to you weakens your spirit and power and will leave your greatest potentials untapped.

It is important to realize that the domains of our lives are not separate. They are intertwined and interdependent on each other. They are the very foundation of the framework of our lives and shape our extended happiness. Just as the frame of the house makes up the home and space in which we live, the framework of what we value makes up the space in which to give our presence and our gifts. Great is the man who honors all the domains of his life and supports their thriving. It makes him complete, whole and incredibly effective. A kiss from his woman's lips in the morning will stay with him all day as he goes out into the world to do his sacred work. We must learn to create harmony and sustainability in all the domains of our life so that we are standing solid foundations for our own fulfillment and happiness. To separate our domains as though they are not connected will cut off an energy flow that is critical.

All our foundations are interdependent while at the same time they are distinct. Even the domains of "relationship" and "relationship(s)" are unique. Your marriage requires a distinctly greater amount of love and attention than your friendships. They are not the same and if treated the same they will suffer. A man who has learned how to create harmony with all the things he values is incredibly dynamic and effective in the world. To balance work and play, spirituality and health, success and intimacy will all feed each other and make a man energized and resourceful. He will access energy that almost seems to be other worldly as he lives a life of purpose and fulfillment. This is critical to the New Man Emerging. Harmony of domains and giving love and attention to what he values is at the core of his gift giving. One is no more important than the other. All are being fed by the same channel of love and commitment. All are equally important knowing that they feed each other and fuel his mission in life.

Take a look at the circle below and either use your book or redraw it for yourself adding other domains that are important to you. Imagine a scale of 1-10, 1 being the closest to the center of the circle and 10 being closest to the outside. 1 represents non-existent or suffering and 10 represents that it couldn't be any better. With a pencil or pen put a dot on each line. For each domain. Where does it fall on the spectrum for you? Once you have all your dots drawn in, connect them all. This will give you a bird's eye view of where you are currently at and what needs attention regarding your fulfillment.

What can you notice about what you drew? Is your circle small and close to the middle where you can notice perhaps you are taking any real risks and playing it safe and small? Or is your circle jagged where some domains are working and others are far too close to the center? Don't judge yourself but notice, what are action steps that you can take immediately to advance your domains, even by an inch?

NME Exercise:

List out all the domains of your life that are important to you. Make sure you have the ones above included. Be honest about where those domains are right now currently for you and take an action on each by the end of the week. If your relationship or marriage needs attention, plan a date. If you haven't been away in a while plan a trip. If your spiritual life is slacking get back to it. Whatever it is for you, make and take actionable steps day-by-day and week-by-week so that each domain is being addressed and the attention that goes to them becomes habitual.

Part 3

The Legacy We Leave

The following year after leaving my father's ashes in his requested open space of Montana, I visited him. It was a commitment that I made to myself that each year I would visit his site and connect with him. It became a time for me to reflect on my year, my accomplishments and even the things I fell short on. I reflected on the year and looked ahead with intention for the year to come. It was a time that I could spend with him like a father and son sharing a cup of coffee.

At first I went out alone, but then after a few days my girlfriend and her friend met me in the area. We fished, explored and I showed them around Montana, the state that my heart so adored. Each corner we turned and explored had so much magic that they were often brought to tears; left speechless and heart filled. They would often joke with me that one of these days they would get a tear out of me. Perhaps I was just used to the beauty of the place or I just got most of my tears out before they arrived. Either way, we made light of it.

On our final day, we had plans to go for a hike that would take up the good portion of the day. I requested that we start out early at sunrise so that I could visit my father's place for the last time until next year. I can remember the sunrise that morning like it was yesterday. It stopped us in our tracks as we drove and forced us to pull off the road and take in the kaleidoscope of colors that the sky was creating that morning. Pinks and blues and clouds that I never saw in my life, all converged on this one area of open sky that longed to be seen. We all sat speechless.

As the sun came up for the day, we were close to my father's place. Still talking and reeling about the sunrise earlier, our spirits were high, as they tended to be each morning. As we approached the area, an area I had been so many times before, I noticed a movement in the brush just near where I enter to see my dad. All of a sudden, within a stone's throw from where I was, stood a giant grizzly bear, up on his hind legs, with a presence that could only remind me of my place in this landscape. His eyes peered through me and I dropped my head and let the tears fall as he disappeared into the nearby brush. I am more than confident that my father's spirit inhabits this place.

Be the Eagle

B eyond our purpose is our legacy. It is the energy we leave
behind even after our bodies are gone and the way we leave
our medicine for those who come after us. Your legacy is in every
life you touch. It requires us to see beyond our limited paradigms,
to gain higher perspectives, not by chance, but by a commitment
to growth and evolution. Thinking how we've always thought will
continue to get us what we've always gotten. Growth demands of us
a rise in our perspective to new heights and taking a higher perspective of what currently is.

In a workshop that I facilitate a few times per year called "The
Masculine Journey," participants are challenged to expand their
visions of their lives, their behaviors and their interpretations on
what it is to be truly masculine. One of my participants came out
of one of the meditations and saw a vision of an eagle flying high
over the mountains. It symbolized to him unlimited possibilities
and where he began to notice where he was holding himself back.
When he shared his insights of his experience I gave him one piece
of feedback that he and I still talk about today. "Rather than watch
the eagle, be the eagle."

Being the eagle is the invitation to live a life from a higher perspective. To be able to see past the mundane and gain a view of life
and others that is outside of our current worldview. To be the eagle
is to commit to expansion that overrides our anxieties of maintaining the status quo.

One of the greatest tools you have to transform your entire life
is your willingness to be wrong about the way that you've got things.

When we have a commitment to be right we are simply strengthening the walls of our box that reinforce our current views and behaviors. The best we gain from this perspective is agreement or disagreement, both of which never lead to or challenge true understanding. The way that you've "got it" isn't bad, it is simply limited. If you don't welcome another perspective then no true dialogue and conversation of growth has any room to expand. We become rigid and positioned on the way we have things and life becomes an inevitable repeating of our views.

Our perspective generates our perception. This means, WHERE we see from generates WHAT we see. The place we see from will give what we look at meaning. For instance, the image below, is that a sunrise or a sunset?

The best you can do is guess. Or perhaps simply make it what you want it to be. Maybe you enjoy sunsets more than sunrises, so that is what you determined it to be. But what if I simply did this...

E

Now, all of a sudden, it is a sunrise. The image never changed, all that was added was the direction of east. Without changing the image at all, the perspective of east gave the image a new meaning. It determined what it was that we were looking at and hence what we see. This is what is meant by our perspective generates our perception.

Our perspectives are not truths, they are places we see and filter the world from and through. Our willingness to be wrong about our filters expands our critical thinking to one that leads to understanding. As human beings, we build our worldview over time and then fight to maintain it. But what we are maintaining is an illusion. Unconsciously, what makes up our paradigm are the limiting beliefs that we have told ourselves about ourselves, others and the world and they have gone unquestioned and unchallenged through a good portion of our lives. The moment we are willing to be wrong or challenge our worldview we open up a space for insight, possibility and new understanding.

The New Man Emerging seeks the perspective of the eagle. He understands that new lands can only be discovered by active exploration. His commitment to growth and journeying new lands begins with the landscape of his own heart and mind. His worldview, like his comfort zone, is elastic and ever growing. He seeks the higher perspective knowing that it will stretch his heart through compassion, forgiveness and understanding as he aims closer and closer to his inner freedom. He knows that staying positioned on being right about the way he has it, will only limit him in the long run and lead to stagnation and lack of growth.

To be the eagle is to be constantly looking inward to a place of personal responsibility that pulls us from a victim perspective in life to a creator role of our lives. Our perspectives aren't truths, they are choices. To choose personal responsibility is to own all of your life; the highs, the lows, the faults and the triumphs. It is to re-empower ourselves that we are in the generating driver's seat of our lives and that we are creating our reality from where and how we choose to see. From the perspective of victim what we see is lack, powerlessness and disappointment. From personal responsibility we see and experience relief, freedom, ownership and power. This is not to state that we are at fault or to blame for the hard events in our lives but rather to see that we have participated in all of it and that by doing so we can adjust our view and interpretation on the past events that we have experienced.

Years ago I met a man in New York City who had the opportunity to meet Gandhi's son several years before. He told me a story that stuck with him and in turn has stuck with me for quite some time. He mentioned a time when his father (Gandhi) had asked his son to take him and one of his assistants to a meeting only a few miles from the ashram. The car needed some servicing so while he and the assistant were at the meeting the son could take the car to the mechanic. After the son dropped the car off for service, he noticed that there was a movie theatre across the street. He decided that while waiting for car to be serviced he would pass the time by seeing a movie. Lost in the film, he didn't realize that it was a double feature and a good amount of time had passed. He quickly raced across the street, grabbed the car and drove to where his father was having his meeting. Noticeably late, he returned to his father and assistant. When asked why he was delayed, Gandhi's son had casually replied that the car took longer than they thought it would. The assistant then mentioned that they called the mechanic quite some time ago and they stated that the car had been ready for quite some time. Blatantly caught in his white lie, he fessed up to his father that he lost track of time while watching a movie. Gandhi listened and instead of responding to his son's admission, he silently refused to get in the car and instead walked the several miles home in silence. The next day, his son, feeling guilty and ashamed, went to Gandhi and begged his father for forgiveness. Gandhi looked at his son and said, "There is nothing to forgive and I am not upset with you at all." His son then asked, "If you weren't upset than why did you refuse to get in the car and be driven home?" To which Gandhi replied, "I didn't get in the car yesterday because I wanted to use the walk home as a meditation. For the several miles of walking I used the time to look deep within myself to see where is it in me that would have my son feel it was better to lie to his father than to tell him the truth."

This story points to personal responsibility, the higher perspective of the eagle. It would be easy to justify his disappointment at his son for lying, but instead Gandhi chose to take ownership of his own participation in his relationship with his son. Making that choice led to opening new doors of love, compassion, forgiveness and personal power. The choice of higher perspective challenges us to grow past our impulsive nature of reaction and calls forth a new mind and heart. It requires our presence to the moment and using our discernment and critical thinking to call forth what we say we want. It stretches our hearts to grow and become responsive to the moment rather than reactive to our past.

To be the eagle is to willingly admit that there is much we don't know. To seek and gain new and higher perspectives that are beyond our current paradigm of thinking. Without having something greater than ourselves we won't take risks and our lives won't change. The moment we seek something greater, give our life over to a vision or a commitment and seek a higher perspective with a willingness to grow, we now have a new place of possibility and power. To be the eagle is to constantly be striving for greater wisdom and depth of living. Higher perspectives challenge us to grow and as we are pulled into the unknown, we develop skills for living that are unavailable to us in our comfort zones.

THE ULTIMATE MEDICINE

If fear is our greatest poison, then forgiveness is our ultimate medicine. Nothing helps us choose a higher perspective and live from a clearer space than forgiveness. It frees us to love, to live and create a new life in every moment.

One of the greatest things that trap us in our past and living a life of limitation is our unwillingness to forgive. To not forgive the past events, people, old behaviors and even ourselves keep us caught to a constant cycle of reaction to moments. We hold energy in our minds and bodies that weakens us and wears us down over time. It debilitates our hearts from truly giving and opening to connection and understanding. It is like swallowing poison hoping that the other person gets sick. It leads to anger and hostility and traps us in our own mind of righteousness and victimhood. The Buddha said "To not forgive is like holding a hot stone waiting to throw it at someone. In the meantime, you are the one getting burned."

As men in our culture have been collectively taught to hold it in and keep it together, they have also concluded that it is stronger and manlier to hold a grudge than to let go, forgive and move on. They interpret forgiveness as a weakness, that to forgive would mean that someone else got the best of them, Believing that to forgive is to condone the other's behavior and somehow have them win while he loses. This is a mistake in thinking and a falsehood that has been perpetuated for too long. Forgiveness is the ultimate medicine because in the end it frees YOU!

Now, I understand that many of us have had some really challenging things happen to us in the past and I say all that I say with sensitivity. When I do workshops for audiences of people I hear some of the most unthinkable things that you can imagine. But I have also seen people have incredible breakthroughs by simply healing the past of what they have let trap them for decades.

The past is over, but to the degree that we re-run it in our minds we become a prisoner to a past that we can no longer control. It shows up in our behavior, habits, thinking, reactions and relationships. It shows itself as anger, hostility, judgment and victimhood and it traps us in mediocrity, at best. We conclude we have no control and we are left powerless to a fate that can pass us by. We think that if we just try harder, do better and compensate for the past than we will somehow forge through to a new beginning and overcome our past. It doesn't work. The power we contain is not in past events themselves, it is how we choose to move forward regardless of what has taken place. In short...

> *It is not about <u>what</u> happened...It is about*
> *what I make what happened, <u>mean</u>.*

Our power is in how we interpret. As human beings we make meaning of things. It is how we compartmentalize the world. But for so many of us, we forget that we are making up meanings to things that are no longer here. Those past events hold significance in our minds that we unconsciously carry out. We live today as though the transgressions of yesterday are still happening; as though, those that hurt us are still hurting us and the wrongs we made yesterday are following us to our death. We must cut the cord of those energetic leashes because that traps us from living today and our future with full potential.

Forgiveness is not a poor pardon or a condoning of behavior. Forgiveness is to love as you did before the transgression; before "it" happened. It is a return to your innocent self that frees you of the mental trappings of regret, anger, victimhood and powerlessness. It is to acknowledge what happened in the past in a neutral way so that the event no longer has power over you. It is to do as the word states, to "for-give" or to "give forward" from a clear space of under-standing. Forgiveness clears space in our hearts and minds and it is the ultimate sign of strength. This is what Gandhi meant when he said "the weak can never forgive. Forgiveness is an attribute of the strong." The strong can say "It happened" and in the next breath say "It no longer matters." The New Man Emerging's life and future is not determined by the past but rather is determined and influenced by what he chooses and how he chooses to be "NOW." Nothing frees that space faster and more effectively than the will-ingness to forgive. To refuse to forgive is what keeps us trapped like prisoners in our own cells forgetting that we are the ones that hold the key. To be free, we must forgive.

Many of us have people and events to forgive. And for others, we ourselves are the ones that we need to turn our forgiveness towards. When we look back on our past, we see how we acted and place a great amount of shame in our actions and transgressions. Some of us are quick to forgive others but find it hard to turn that action towards ourselves. Either way, we remain trapped. To not offer for-giveness to ourselves will ultimately have us repeat old behaviors that no longer work and stunt our growth as we attempt to move forward.

Consider for a moment, that you are asked to build a house but you are only given half of the tools. You could still build something but it would not be optimum. Then, years later, you were given all the proper tools and asked to build a house again. With your previ-ous experience and a greater set of tools you could build a far better home. It would be unwise not to use the new tools and to try and build a better house with the old tools only. This is what forgiveness offers. The tools are your new consciousness. To look back on your past and to realize that you built the best that you could with the tools you had access to at the time. Now is new. And you are new with a new set of tools, insights and consciousness. With forgive-ness and what you have access to now, you can build something far greater. It is up to you to free yourself of the past and use what you have now so that you can create a greater future for yourself and others.

When I was in fourth grade my teacher taught my class how to catch a monkey. I was astonished by the simplicity of it the technique. I never forgot it. Years later I was in southern India spending time traveling and was in an ashram village under the sacred mountain of Arunachala where the sage, Ramana Maharshi had become self-realized. As I spent time there I noticed the monkeys and how they seemed to overrun the small town. I recalled the story of when I was young and asked one of the locals if my understanding of how to catch a monkey was correct. He was amused that I knew the trick.

To catch a monkey they simply tie a rope to a tree or pole and attached a closed, six-sided box to the rope. They carve out a small hole and inside the box they place one banana. The hole that they carve is big enough for the monkey, with an empty fist, to squeeze its hand into. Once the monkey then grabs the banana and makes a fist, the hole is too small for the monkey to get its hand out of with a fist and the banana. There is no trap, no trigger, no switch, and no lock. The monkey is actually trapping itself. Forgetting that there is an entire jungle of bananas that the monkey has access to, the monkey stays committed to being right that THIS banana is his and instead traps himself. To be free, all the monkey would need to do is, simply, let go, and drop the banana.

We laugh at the monkey that it traps itself. But as human beings we are incredibly similar. We get committed to all the reasons we can't be free. All the past stories and trappings keep us locked in our paradigm and worldview that limits us and keep us stuck. We scream "This is my banana!!!" and we get committed to all the belief systems that we construct to make ourselves right about who we are and what we are worthy of. It is time to let it go. It is time to drop the banana and to free ourselves from our self-created shackles. It is up to us and it is time.

The door that keeps us trapped was never locked. We only imagined that it was. To be free, we must forgive ourselves and others and our past. In doing so, we create a space of possibility that was inaccessible before our choice to let it go. Without forgiveness, we remain trapped and stuck in belief systems that have us recreate old behaviors that give us the same lackluster results. We remain unconsciously stuck when we don't forgive. We build imaginary walls around our heart and mind that has us duplicate our limits over and over again. Until we consciously remove the bricks from those walls we will never have access to our true nature and the power that it offers us.

Forgiveness is a choice, one of the most powerful choices we can ever make. The past is done. It is gone. The only power we have over it is how we choose to view it. Was what happened designed to trap us or to free us? Depending on how you choose to view it, it will keep you stuck or propel you forward. To forgive is one of the ultimate acts of courage and strength. It is at the heart and foundation of the New Man Emerging. It is our power and our choice, one that we get to make freely and often.

NME Exercise:
List out all the grievances you have with yourself and with others and past events. Next to each list what holding on to those grievances is costing you, i.e. Peace, freedom, love, connection etc. Then, once you have taken your time with this process build a fire. Light some sage and close your eyes and take a few deep breaths. When you are ready, put your grievances in the fire, either all together or one at a time. Let the fire burn away everything that limits you.

FIND YOUR TRIBE

*"The strength of the pack is the wolf and the
strength of the wolf is the pack."*
— Rudyard Kipling

Today, perhaps more than ever, men are desperately seeking brotherhood and belonging. It is becoming more prevalent and obvious that isolation creates disease. And its remedy is connection. Isolated and disconnected, we will do incredibly harmful things to others and ourselves. With a sense of connection we develop a safety and significance that only comes with being part of a tribe.

Part of the success of the human species is based on the fact that by nature, we are a tribal species. To have family and a support system as we grow and learn is one of the most vital aspects our emotional needs as people. Our ancestors gathered around fires, told stories and taught lessons and ate together as part of their daily rituals. Boys were raised not only by their fathers but also by grandfathers, uncles and elders. There was no shortage masculine influence and guidance. Men retreated with other men and learned the ways of warriors, sages and protectors. There were rites of passage that boys experienced that were different from girls. For the girls it was physical, their first period was a distinct moment in time that they could reference that moved than from girlhood into womanhood. For boys, there needed to be deliberate rituals designed so that they could understand and directly relate to the journey from boyhood into manhood. First hunts, vision quests, even wartime were ways that boys transitioned. Today, our rites of passage for boys are gone, or at least seemingly dangerous like the first time we get drunk, laid or get into a fight. The spiritual component to our boys' growth seems lost and hence we are creating disconnected and isolated men, confused with how to relate with themselves and other men.

The Industrial Revolution became a major shift in the father-son relationship of our countries male emotional evolution. Before then, boys often spent most of their days with their fathers, learning their craft and being an apprentice to their father's mentorship. Boys watched their dads farm and spent time with them in the fields. Or they grew up in their fathers shop learning the craft of their father that financially provided for their family. Hours of each day were spent in the presence of their masculine influence. And while learning a craft they were also learning the traits of men directly from their fathers. In Robert Bly's book, "Iron John," he cites the Industrial Revolution as a huge turning point in our species and a major shift in the family dynamic, especially between fathers and sons. During the time, and after, men were far less likely to earn their living by a craft and instead began going off to work for companies and corporations. This was a huge departure from the norm at that time and the amount of time boys and fathers interacted greatly decreased. Boys began being raised predominantly by their mothers and female influences and fathers were absent in the child raising process due to work. This may seem subtle or even a necessary sacrifice for the sake of progress, but what Bly proposes is that boys began to distrust their fathers and other men due to lack of presence in their lives.

From this perspective, this is a major blemish on the masculine psyche. Lack of trust in other men at the core of a man will have him isolate and build walls around his heart with other men. In turn, he will cut himself off from the opportunity to gather with men in a healthy and healing way. The challenges of men and women are equal, but not the same and for men there is a great healing that arises when we retreat and connect. There is a magic that is present when men gather around a fire, whether literal or metaphoric. And men need to learn to trust their brothers in order to get to the true heart of healing the masculine spirit.

The idea of the "self-made man," and the man that "goes it alone" is as prevalent in our culture as it is detrimental. It leaves men thinking that they must handle their problems as well as achieve their successes solely on their own. It goes against the nature of tribal support and significance within a community. It has us isolate and cut off our spirits and gifts to our brothers and leaves us in a competitive reflex. Competition on a ball field can generate achievement and sportsmanship. Competition for human needs and emotional wellbeing creates greed and selfishness.

Men that have served in battle together, achieved sport accolades on a team or sweat together in a cause, know the importance of relying on each other. The brotherhood and kinship experienced in hard or traumatic times heightens an awareness of the human spirit that cannot be experienced in isolation. "Tribes" by Sebastian Junger reveals a deep understanding of how so many soldiers struggle returning to civilian life due to the contrast of active duty of course, but also a deep sense of obligation and loss of leaving their brothers behind. To go from such an intense state of connection to alone in society becomes a traumatic shock to their emotional state.

As men, we must begin to break down the emotional barriers we've built between one another. We are obligated to heal the masculine spirit of mistrust of other men and finally realize the power of vulnerability, of sharing and of support. This is not weakness, this is strength and we must once again remember the power that comes through a sense of belonging.

If you do not have a tribe, you must find them. And do it quickly. A man committed to his best self needs a group of men that will encourage him as well as hold his feet to the fire. Having a group that is willing to give and receive honest feedback is crucial to growth and potential. We all have blind spots and shortcomings and to be able to have a tribe of eyes and hearts to help you course correct is vital to living fully. Find your tribe and find them now.

There is a saying "that you are the average of the five people you spend the most time with." If you want to know someone, look around them at who they hang out with consistently. Audit your commodities. Are you spending your time with people desiring to grow and be the best versions of themselves or are you spending energy on people satisfied with the status quo? Are you giving your commodities to people cultivating a life of fulfillment or are you surrounded by naysayers, victims to life and men acting as boys? Are the people in your life encouraging you to go after your dreams or are they reminding you why your dreams are impossible? These are not easy questions to ask, however, they still demand your honesty. This may require deep introspection and some challenging conversations of boundaries and intentional growth. And yet, it is incredibly necessary. You will only get so far on your own and you must be vigilant about who gets, or in many cases who depletes, your energy.

To be clear, your tribe is not the boys you go drinking with, frat brothers from college or men you feel obliged to hang out with because you have a history and grew up together. Some of them may be part of your tribe but just because you have history doesn't automatically give them admission. Your tribe are the people you trust to give you honest feedback, men that you are comfortable opening up to vulnerably, men that won't run at the first sign of your shortcomings and your shadow self. It is a group that holds each other accountable to their vision, their principles and their deepest desires. It is a group of modern day warriors that are committed to slaying the demons of their own minds and hearts. Their brother's victory is their victory and vice versa. Too often, men do not have this dynamic in their life and we suffer because of it. The model of "go-it-alone" has men closed off to trust and connection with other men because from this model that is seen as a sign of weakness.

There is no getting to the mountaintop alone!

The idea that you do anything on your own is a myth and one worth getting rid of immediately. If you want to achieve anything in life as fast and efficiently as possible, build a team. What we do and can do together far exceeds what we can do alone. It is vital to have a tribe if you want to reach your true potential.

Along with men you trust that are honorable and integrity driven, you also want to have men in three positions of mentorship within your tribe. First, you want to have a mentor. A man that you look up to, learn from, are guided by and navigate based on your admiration for. These are our elders, the men that are examples to us on how to live and love as true men. Hire a coach or someone that you have admiration for and connect with them on a routine basis. Our ancestors revered our elders as guides and sign posts on how to live a dignified life. That role has shifted dramatically in our current culture and it is leaving men lost and confused on how to purposefully navigate their future. This role is incredibly important, especially for men without fathers or grandfathers that feel as though there is no one of wisdom and guidance they can turn to.

This isn't necessarily a conversation about age. If wisdom came with age than everyone older than us would all be sages. That's clearly not the case. This position in your tribe is about someone that fits the elder role to you due to admiration and example even if they are younger than you in age.

Second, you must have men alongside you in your tribe. These are your compatriots, your equals and your fellow warriors. These are the men that are at equal pace to you on your journey. Perhaps you are up to a similar vision or goal, you are age equivalent or simply at the same seasons of life. These are the men that you are in the trenches with, so to speak. These men will drive you through healthy competition and push you to move passed your comfort zone while feeling encouraged and supported. They are essential. They will do the most to reflect you back to yourself because they are in the most similar situations of life. You will learn most from them what is working and what is not. Seek their feedback and make adjustments accordingly.

Third, to be most fulfilled, you need to be a mentor to other men. You must have a roster of men that seek your council. Men that come to you for advice and guidance. These are the learners. These are the men that are now where you used to be in life and due to your commitment to growth you now have tools and strategies to pass on to the men who follow behind you. These men are seeking you and they need you. You can't only be receiving from your elders and competing with your equal companions without contributing to the men coming up the ranks.

To truly be fulfilled you must contribute what you have learned and give it generously to all that follow. This is where true legacy is given. This is the space where you leave a lasting mark on the future; even after you are gone. Acquire all that you can in this life and then freely give it back to all those earnestly seeking what you have learned. This is true fulfillment and legacy.

Your tribe is critical to your growth and progress as a New Man Emerging. It is a sense of strength and safety that is as valuable today as gold. To go without, it is to do yourself and other men a disservice to potential and fulfillment. I dedicate a portion of my business to building tribes among men so that they can once again experience the magic of when men gather around a fire. It is one of my greatest pleasures to see men reconnect with their spirit while forming bonds of brotherhood that will last a lifetime. The age of lone wolf is over, if it was ever really here or effective. The time for brotherhood and connection will be the difference for our future of boys and men. They get to remember that they are not alone in this great big world but rather they have a tribe and they are capable and worthy of a sense of belonging.

NME Exercise:

#1 - FIND YOUR TRIBE! There are countless groups and forums today that are dedicated to men connecting. Research and join one this week.

#2 - Look at the three positions of tribe in your life. Do you have at least one or more in each position of elder, compatriot and learner?

Are there certain people that you know fit the roles but you haven't reached out and connected to them lately? Do it, do it today.

If you are lacking in these roles seek to build them up immediately. Hire a coach, create accountability roles with colleagues or people you are equal with and let people behind you know you are available to them if they need you.

THE LION AND THE FOX

*"I don't want my life to be defined by what is etched on
a tombstone. I want it to be defined by what is etched
in the lives and hearts of those I've touched."*
— Steve Maraboli

*"There was a man in South India. He wanted to pursue a
spiritual path. In India, pursuing spiritual path means, it's
a natural habit, first thing is - they will go out into the forest,
looking for a cave to sit and meditate. So the man went off to
the jungle, but of course you position yourself close to the village, because you need food. So he sat there and started mantra.
Whenever he got hungry, he came to the village got some food and
went back. And as night fell he noticed there was a fox, both his
front legs were severed by some trap or something and they were
gone, but still he was well fed and healthy. Nature is not kind to
any kind of incapability. If you lose your legs, you lose your life.
But this fox has lost its legs but was well fed and healthy. He was
surprised. But then, he ignored it and focused on his meditation.
As night fell he heard the roar of a lion coming, he forgot about
his meditation and climbed up a tree. He sat there and for his
amazement, the lion, a full grown male lion came with a piece
of meat and brought it and dropped it in front of the fox and
went away. The fox had its dinner. He couldn't believe this. A
crippled fox is being fed by a furious lion. Hallelujah. This is a
miracle. This is a message from the divine. What is it? What is it?
What is it? And he was wondering and wondering and the next*

evening the lion came again with a piece of meat, dropped it in front of the fox and went away. Now he thought - for sure this is a message god is sending to me. What is it? Then he interpreted it in his own way. He said: "Even an injured fox in this forest is being fed by a lion, you fool, what are you going looking for food for, just sit here and it will come and fall in your mouth". So he simply sat. One day, two days, three days, meditation became more like a struggle, fourth day even more, by the seventh day he was starving, he was between life and death. Another yogi was passing that way, he heard these sounds of a man dying, and he came down and asked: "What happened to you, why are you in this condition?" The starving man said: "Oh yogi, please tell me. A divine message came to me, I went by the message and I became like this". The yogi asked: "What happened? The starving man said: "Look there, there is an injured fox, every day that fox is being fed by a furious lion, is this not God's message to me, is this not a divine message?" The yogi looked at him and said: "Definitely this is a divine message, but why is it that you chose to be like an injured fox and not like a generous lion?"

— Sadhguru

Your potential and possibility is astounding, if you would only just claim it. For decades we have been taught to downplay our wants, to dim our light and our gifts and to be satisfied with the status quo. We are taught to come down to earth and be satisfied with the norm. But why accept the crumbs of life when you are capable of and deserve the whole loaf? To the New Man Emerging, mediocrity will never do. His drive is to excel and experience excellence in all the domains of his life. To balance the challenges of work, woman, passion and responsibility and have them all succeed. He is not seeking to be better than his fellow man but rather so he can be a contribution and a blueprint example for the men that follow. The New Man Emerging lives by his vision and deeper than that he is called to a legacy. To create something in this world that lives on after him. This is beyond his children and his last name. It lives deeper in his heart, his medicine, and his purpose. And it is what calls him forth, even in his darkest and unsure moments. It beckons him deep in his soul, even when it makes absolutely no sense logically. It is to live from the place of his soul and be willing to forgo anything that hinders his deeper growth.

If we shrink when we are faced with challenges, accept the bare minimum and maintain the status quo, we are hurting ourselves and also the men that come after us. If we continue to default to what is familiar, then we will continue to get what we have always gotten. But if we choose to truly make a difference in our own lives and communities and make a lasting dent in infinity, then it will require from us to become a whole new man. Every phase of growth in our lives will require a whole new us. That is why, now, we are emerging. We are becoming a new version of ourselves, both individually and collectively. This moment in time is calling forth the best version of who we are as men. The call is here, the time is now. Will you answer it?

The choice is yours; to be the injured fox or the generous lion. Will you continue to withhold the gifts that you have been given, accept "good enough" and blend in to the status quo? Or, will you regain your inner kingdom and live from a place of contribution, generosity and influence? The choice is ours and it has always been. For too long we have waited and procrastinated away our life and power. Now is the time to reclaim a life that is truly worth living and dying for. You were never meant to be average; the world was created for you to use it as a canvas to a life you have always imagined.

No one can stop you but you.

LIVE BY OUR PROMISES

A great and honorable man is measured by the promises that he keeps. To live by our promises is to put action to our desires and allow us to be shaped by them. As we do, we allow the hands of life to shape us from inside us rather than external forces and conditions dictating our state and what occurs in our life. To follow through on our promises is to build trust, respect and dependability in others as well as generating self-esteem in ourselves.

Average men live by circumstances and conditions, great men live by commitments. Too often men hope or wish their lives to be a certain way but fail to see the passivity in their wanting. They state to life and the universe their preferences and abandon them the moment challenge and adversity arise. The myth of "one day" and the language of "Wouldn't it be nice if…" keeps them trapped in a tepid pool of mediocrity, hoping and wishing that if life somehow throws them a bone that they will ultimately utilize it, once it shows up. The New Man Emerging doesn't wait for this to happen. He speaks his life into existence with the technology of language. He declares his life be so and so it is. He understands that his promises are declarations of assurance that he will make what he desires happen. He is not molded by his circumstances externally but rather shaped by his commitment to follow through on what he declares to himself and others.

Hoping requires luck, promising requires action. The moment we speak our promise to life, others and ourselves we are at the starting point and nothing is valued or gained until it comes to fruition. When we declare our promises to be kept, we in that moment, allow the journey to shape us so that they become so. The constant shifting and shaping of our word evolves the very fabric of who we are.

Language is a technology. It is a vibrational aspect of creation. Our thoughts are creative, but they gain power the moment we speak them. To declare and promise something so is to generate from a space of possibility that allows us to shape our potential future. Just as our principles guide and organize our inner world, our promises shape and guide our outer world and our relationships with others. They are the frameworks in which we create our future. Our word is our bond and becomes our greatest currency of exchange to ourselves and to others. When we keep our promises, we generate trust and respect and when we break them we diminish our power to effectively create.

To give our word and keep our promises to others produces the experience that they matter and that who they are to us is important. When we break our promises to others, however small, we generate the experience that they are insignificant and that outer circumstances are more important than our commitments to them. We devalue others and ourselves by breaking our promises. In Steven Covey's book "The 7 Habits of Highly Effective People," he equates our word to an emotional bank account. This means that every time we give our word to someone or our self and keep it, it is equivalent to making a deposit into our self-esteem. Every time we break our promise, to our self or to another, is to make a withdrawal from our self-esteem. Over time, as we make or break promises, it directly relates to how well we interpret our own self-worth and our capabilities.

When we give our word and keep it there is a process of completion, seeing something through to the end that naturally begins to strengthen our effectiveness. We begin to remember our own capability and power to declare and create from our word to our action and seeing it all the way through.

Every time we break our promises to ourselves, our spouses, our children, friends and colleagues we diminish our standing in our own life. We forget the power of our promises and the next time we show up we feel reduced and a touch less capable. It alters our relationship with others over time, broken promise by broken promise. We become conditioned to think that our word is not as important and that our integrity is not something that we can control. The New Man Emerging disagrees. He understands that his word is his currency and his promises to himself and others directly reflect his own integrity.

Our spouses and our children don't care about our checklists and deadlines. They care about us being our word to each other. To make money and meet deadlines while losing our integrity in the process is a disservice to everyone in our lives. When we say we will be on time, watch the kids game, do what we said we would and we don't we are left with excuses that don't matter. We build our relationships up to exceptional by follow through, not by excuses. Excuse by excuse chips away at all our self-esteem and leaves us altered. We must learn to put our word first and live by our commitments rather than our excuses.

Does this mean we must be perfect? Can we never break our word or never give it for fear of falling short? Certainly not. We must learn to live in dichotomy, two seemingly opposite views coexisting simultaneously. We must live our life as though we will never break our word and promises, all the while realizing that integrity is a mountaintop that will never be reached. There is always another level of excellence that awaits us. If you are wearing skin, there is more work to do.

Our word has lost social value, but it has not lost its effectiveness. It is time to regain our worth through the vehicle of our word. No prescription for esteem will ever be written that is more potent than the relationship that we create with what we say we will do and then do it. For some of us, we have spent decades breaking our word to others and ourselves. Doing so has altered relationships and their value and insidiously, lack of worth has built a home in our hearts and minds. To rid it, start now. Be your word in all you say you will do and watch self-esteem climb. If you break your word, acknowledge it, clean it up and move forward.

When we live by our promises we access creativity, value, power, honor, trust and respect. These become the food for the soul of the New Man Emerging. To be fed by his own principles and follow through action, becomes his basic and routine way of operating. It builds a foundation in his life where he is effective and where people feel valued and safe around him. He holds his word as his bond and people know its extraordinary value.

When we build self-esteem through living by our promises we then begin to believe our own promises again. We begin to clearly see our vision and value in life. We can declare great and exceptional things in life and know deep down in our core that they are possible. Our promises reshape us out of our comfort zones into a life of extraordinary value. Below is a manifesto I wrote years ago that I look at each day in my office to remind me to live by my promises, to create value in the world and to believe that it is all possible.

I will do my very best in all the circumstances and areas of my life. I will own my gifts and talents and unendingly give them to the world. *I will stoke the fire of the unique passion that God put in my heart.* I will admit to myself and others my shortcomings and never pretend I am more than what is true. I WILL BE SLOW TO JUDGE AND QUICK TO FORGIVE. <u>I will surround myself with people that build me up, encourage me, support me and respectfully challenge me to be my very best.</u> *I WILL LET THE FIRE OF SELF INQUIRY BURN AWAY EVERYTHING I AM NOT.* I will learn from those ahead of me, challenge those beside me and support those who follow. **I will make of this life a DARING and BOLD Adventure.** I will stay open, honest, authentic and willingly walk into the uncomfortable space of vulnerability. I will <u>get up,</u> <u>show up</u> and <u>step up</u>. *I will protect my family and loved ones, both physically and spiritually.* <u>*I will honor the past, be grateful for the present and believe in the future.*</u> *I will love, protect and serve the women in my life.* I will respect and honor my brothers and the paths they fight for. *I will treat the earth with reverence and respect and be mindful* **of the generations to come.** I will stand up when I see injustice - stand out when I see conformity - sit down when the stage is not mine - speak up when voices go unheard. *I wiLL Laugh at myseLf and my mIstaKes.* <u>I will fail, succeed and fail again because that is my surest way to growth.</u> **I will love, I will cry, I will laugh.** I will treat my mind and body with respect. I will nourish it when hungry, rest it when tired and move it when it seeks strength. **I will not waste time,** I will treat it like a *TREASURE* and use it to drive me to leave nothing undone.

I will leave a legacy. I will not die until I have changed the world...

NME Exercise:

1) *What are your promises? What are the things you have given your word to yourself and to others? Are you following through? If not, why not? What are you allowing to get in your way? Notice yourself and make any necessary adjustments*

needed. Reach out to people that you have failed to follow through with and let them know that you acknowledge that you didn't come through; own it. Let them know what you are committed to as you move forward together.

2) *Create a manifesto. Something that you can look at (like above) each day so that you can be reminded of why you are here on earth and that you value what it is that you promise to yourself and others.*

QUESTION #2

I live my life knowing that one day it will end. That one day I will return to the place of my origin. I will remember the divinity within me and see the perfection of all that was laid out before me in my life, even if I couldn't see it for myself. I live my life doing my best to answer question #1, "How well did you tend to that unique fire that I put in your heart?" It is a question that fuels me as well as haunts me. Will I be able to answer it truthfully and whole-heartedly? Am I doing enough to meet the question full heart and head on? Am I doing enough? Period. When I stress or worry about the future, when I sell myself or my gifts short and try to convince myself that there is still a mountain top to be reached and then and only then will God deem me worthy, I think of question #2 and it puts me back at ease. When I die, like an old friend returning from a long and arduous trip that is excited that I am home safe, God will simply ask me, "How was heaven?"

This is the question that has me reframe this life. Through all the challenges and growth spurts, all the uncertainty and chaos of the world, this question has me remember the enormous and unspeakable beauty that is contained in this world and this life. The landscapes and natural beauty contained on this earth are immeasurable and the landscapes of the human heart were well worth the admission. The fact that we are breathing, right now in this instant, is a divine miracle. That our hearts beat and blood flows and each day, we get to wake up and create something extraordinary truly would be the definition of heaven. The exception here is that we have a choice.

We have a choice to make this heaven or hell, mundane or magnificent. Every day we have an opportunity to live and love to a depth that has not yet been reached. Or we can give in to fear and justify why we continue to close off our hearts. We can enjoy this planet that we live on and make it something we are proud to leave our next generations or we can continue to mistreat it and lose out on its wonder and natural beauty by being greedy, selfish and shortsighted.

There is more than enough that has been provided to us on this earth that no one needs to go hungry, that all can be fed and healthy and that we can all experience dignity while living in harmony with nature and our earth. To ask for more when we die seems strange when we have mistreated all that we have been given here. Often times when I sit with my loved ones I silently say to myself and sometimes out loud, "How dare I ask for more?" If we were truly present to the magic of this moment, we would all be on our knees in gratitude. The New Man Emerging isn't waiting for heaven; he is creating it, here and now.

The obstacles are great, there is no doubt. We have poisoned our home, our waters and our land. We have hurt each other and ourselves. We've looked through the lens of scarcity for too long and thought only about this immediate moment and rarely practiced prudence and patience for the generations after us. We have shaken our fists at the heavens and waited for signs and answers when they are here already, encoded into the very fabric of who we are. We must not delay any longer. We must wake up to the fact that what we need, we have. All it requires is that we accept it and trust it, and each other.

The greatest obstacle that we face in making home our heaven is and always has been the same, ourselves. What we have done to one and other is often times inconceivable. It has us close our hearts and attempt to get through life as little unscathed as possible; never really living to our fullest potential because the possibility of the worst outcome seems too daunting. What we have done to each other in the name of scarcity, greed and the need to be right is heartbreaking and gasping.

"To her fair works did Nature link
The human soul that through me ran;
And much it grieved my heart to think
What man has made of man."
— William Wordsworth

But all is not lost. There is hope. There is you! The New Man Emerging. A man that sees the possibility in life and sees passed the façade of fear in his brother's eyes and practices the ultimate medicine of forgiveness. A man willing to let go of what once was for the dream of what could be. As the masculine awakens, we will be able to create a new dream. It is a dream where we all walk with dignity and honor, not only for ourselves but all of humanity. We can remember that there is enough for us all to be fulfilled. This vision is beyond politic, race and even religion. It is the vision of the true human spirit that goes beyond ideology and connects to the core of the human spirit, once again making home, heaven, and heaven, home.

One day a man said to God, "God, I would like to
know what Heaven and Hell are like."

God showed the man two doors. Inside the first one, in the middle of the
room, was a large round table with a large pot of stew. It smelled delicious
and made the man's mouth water, but the people sitting around the table
were thin and sickly. They appeared to be famished. They were holding
spoons with very long handles and each found it possible to reach into
the pot of stew and take a spoonful, but because the handle was longer
than their arms, they could not get the spoons back into their mouths.

The man shuddered at the sight of their misery and suf-
fering. God said, "You have seen Hell."

Behind the second door, the room appeared exactly the same. There was
the large round table with the large pot of wonderful stew that made

the man's mouth water. The people had the same long-handled spoons, but they were well nourished and plump, laughing and talking.

The man said, "I don't understand."

God smiled. It is simple, he said, "Love only requires one skill. These people learned early on to share. In heaven, we feed one another."
— Author Unknown

The time of "survival of the fittest" is coming to an end. We are now entering the time of the survival of the most "cooperative." True evolution favors the whole organism, not the individual cell. When we remember to feed each other, we will remember that we are all one organism, one family, one tribe. This is not a call to sameness but a call to remembering our highest selves through one another. We all are significant and we all possess unique medicine.

Many tribes of North and South America believed that wealth was not determined by how much you accumulated, but rather by how much you gave away. It was called, Anyi. And it was the ultimate statement of generosity. Contrary to our current culture, true success is actually in what we contribute rather than in what gain in goods or status. If we have much, we have much to give.

What it will take is for us to awaken to a new possibility. We must be willing to risk the pain of smallness for the promise of new opportunity and the growth that comes in between and to make our values, principles and vision our aiming mission in life and fuel our honor and integrity as food on our fire. We aim at a world that we can all be proud of, where we all walk with dignity. And you would be one of the people that created it. You played your part, you wrote your verse.

When we feed each other, we break free of the shackles of scarcity and not enough-ness and we reinforce a sense of connection and belonging that has been dormant within us for long enough. As we live and give from this place we remember a simple truth, that **as we raise each other up, we too are lifted in the process.** We have the opportunity each day to create this, to let our medicine speak through us and to create a world that works, for everyone.

This is true giving. To give of ourselves with all that we have of this life. This is to die on empty, with all our gifts given. This life is our gift. May we be fortunate enough to live with an un-payable debt. One that calls forth our purpose to give and stretch our lives into expanded possibilities. So that when we die, we die as free men, with only love in our hearts and thank you on our lips.

Goodbye, for Now

*"What is life?... It is the breath of a buffalo in the wintertime. It is the
little shadow which runs across the grass and loses itself in the sunset."*
— Crowfoot, Blackfoot Nation

Our time together is limited. We are a speck of dust in the
sands of time. But with that, we are also powerful. We have
the opportunity each day to wake up and make a dent in infinity.
We are gifted with the unlimited possibility of a future that has
not been written yet. Human beings are not a fixed reality; we can
adjust our lives in an instant if we so choose. Contrary to what most
believe, our lives are not determined by our past. Our lives and our
future are determined and influenced by what we choose and how
we choose to be, NOW! We are blessed with the opportunity to live
anew and to create a world that works, for everyone.

The New Man Emerging sees his part in this and he lives
into it, willingly, responsibly and unapologetically. He sees his
place in the great mystery of life and embraces the opportunity
to serve to the best of his ability with grace, power and gratitude. He remembers that through service to others he remembers himself. There is a great role to play and it will require the
consciousness of men with honor and dignity to live it out so that
we are once again reminded that heaven is here and now, if we
only choose it.

In the Bible, the first question man ever asks God, after Cain
kills Able, is simply this, "Am I my brother's keeper?" Interestingly
enough, God never answers the question. God lets us figure it out

for ourselves. For generations we have answered that question with a resounding "no." We've decided that our lives are about ourselves and perhaps the people closest to us, only. In the times that we have answered no, we have suffered. We have forgotten that we are connected to something far greater than ourselves. And we have paid prices for it. We have systematically destroyed our earth, the very home in which we live. We have deteriorated trust between men and women and we have forgotten how to praise and support each other. We have divided each other based on belief systems rather than connect our hearts through our shared humanness. We have warred with each other, wronged each other and robbed each other of basic freedom, dignity and human rights.

When we answer the question "Am I my brother's keeper?" with a collective "Yes!" then that will be the moment we begin to remember who we are. It will be the moment where forgiveness clears the space of who we thought we were and how we believed we needed to act. It will clear the space for a new possibility; one of hope, of purpose and of peace. We will once again remember that we are connected far beyond agree and disagree, beyond our limited perceptions of ourselves and life and we will again awake from the slumber that we put ourselves in. Human beings live in a cage forgetting the door was never locked. The way out is through our inner world of reclaiming our place in nature, with ourselves and with each other. When we learn to "feed each other" we will once again remember our connection to one another and to our purpose and to our divine origin.

> *If we have no peace, it is because we have forgot-*
> *ten that we belong to each other."*
> — Mother Theresa

This is the journey. And the journey never ends. Books conclude but the chapters of life are never finished. There is a New

Man Emerging. And he is an example to all those who come after him. He demonstrates a life of purpose, passion, freedom and fulfillment. Not only that they are possible in his life, but also in fact they are the God given right of every man, if he so chooses to live it. It is the path of the true human being. It is a path of wholeness, where head and heart are married as one and used to serve a mission far greater than his fear. It is a path that requires strength and fortitude, patience and humility, love and grace. On this path, the masculine heart is healed and the boy can rest knowing that the man in him his enough. The leader can emerge as free, courageous and inspiring beyond measure. The fire within is fueled with love and beauty and as he awakens the world is transformed into a possibility that we have not yet experienced collectively. This journey takes us from the battlefield of our minds to the safe and secure rooms of our hearts. And as we make this journey, we heal together. The journey never ends, the fire never goes out.

There is a New Man Emerging. You are that man. You are on this journey.

And it is good.

A'ho